ADVICE

TO THE

STUDENT OF FRENCH

by

R. C. KNIGHT

M.A. (Oxon.), D. ès L.
*Professor of French in the University
College of Swansea*

F. W. A. GEORGE

B.A., Ph.D. (London)
*Lecturer in French in the University
College of Swansea*

OXFORD
BASIL BLACKWELL
1960

© BASIL BLACKWELL, 1960

First edition 1955
Reprinted 1960

PRINTED IN GREAT BRITAIN
BY A. T. BROOME AND SON, ST. CLEMENT'S, OXFORD

PREFACE

The first impression of this book met with generous encouragement from our colleagues. Their two main criticisms were not unjust. The sections on philology, linguistics and Old French literature are more detailed than the rest (this we thought needful because they are uncharted territory for the freshman); and the demands are made to seem so heavy as to be perhaps discouraging. Well, the demands are not ours, and if they are perfectionist it may be no bad thing to stress the unfashionable virtues of work, and especially reading, to future Arts students. If a few lazy ones are scared off in time, that is all to the good. The rest may remember that University courses are designed to enable suitable candidates to pass in normal circumstances. And we do point out that no course includes more than a selection of the specialisms we describe.

Our aim was to put down the most important of the things that all successful students find out, but sometimes not before valuable time has been wasted. We write more particularly for those just beginning, or still waiting to begin, a University course in French. Our advice concerns in the first place the intensive ' single Honours ' course, but it applies as well, omitting what may be irrelevant, to ' Joint Honours ', ' subsidiary ' and ' pass ' courses. It is written with the modern Universities of England and Wales in mind—Oxford and Cambridge organize studies differently, and of the Scottish system we are not competent to speak. But we believe the principles are those that should govern the study of any language and its literature, anywhere.

F. W. A. George was principally responsible for the sections on language and medieval literature, and R. C. Knight for most of the rest. We are indebted to several friends and colleagues, and most of all to Mr. J. Killa Williams, M.A., lecturer in French in the University College of Wales, Aberystwyth, for very helpful criticism and suggestions. In this re-impression we have taken the opportunity to remove a few blemishes and make a few changes in the bibliography.

CONTENTS

INTRODUCTION

What are you letting yourself in for ?

The purpose of an Honours school is to make people competent over a wide intellectual field by making them cultivate one limited patch intensively; for you cannot go deep in any subject without touching most of the rest. French studies are an education on several levels. You learn to write French (and, of course, to speak it—but if this is what you want most you can achieve it more quickly elsewhere); you read books in French; you thus gain some idea how Frenchmen think, feel or have done in the past, and what France has given the world, in thought, in literature, and in the other arts too. Meanwhile the contact should make you more responsive to thought and to beauty in general, so that whatever you read, and much else of what you see and hear, means more to you in future. At the same time, by practical and theoretical study of one language, you should become more sensitive to language in general, and more skilled in its use—your own language at least as much as French.

Language and literature are separate branches requiring different kinds of aptitude; but it is right to link them, for each needs the other's help, and each starts from the same matter—words and their use.

In language, the familiar routine of proses and translations will take on new interest and meaning as it takes its place in the study of one of the most fascinating and wonderful of human activities, speech—an activity to be appreciated (and practised) as an art, and investigated by the methods of science, psychology, and history.

In literature, the ideal would be to explore the whole panorama of French writing since its beginnings, with all that helps to explain it. But this is impossible, for there is too much : ' outlines ' are not knowledge, and how much you do achieve will depend on whether you can really get inside your first few set books, and grasp and feel all that they have to convey to you. A

5

student of literature who cannot do this is a blind man discussing colours; and it takes time and labour. When the art of reading is mastered broader views are possible, but not before.

Add to this varying doses of initiation into the other arts as practised in France, the history and the ' civilization ' of France. All these aspects will be discussed in the pages that follow, but first a few words about the spirit in which you approach your study, and the methods you need to use.

Do not expect it to be easy. It will be unrewarding grind unless you are attracted to the subject; and if you are, it will be exacting work which will grow more exacting as your powers develop. It demands abilities you still have to acquire—of which you only showed the promise when you were accepted by your French department, however brilliant the scholarship you may have won. It involves learning new ways of learning, and perhaps unlearning old ones.

' Learning ' still includes committing facts to memory—I say ' still ', though some students seem to have avoided doing this even at school : so much the worse for them. But the facts you will be given, and the more numerous facts you will be expected to go and find out, are not all to be memorized, and none of them (except irregular verbs, and perhaps not these) are only to be memorized—they are to be compared, combined, interpreted. The result of this process, which involves thought, is what is properly called learning. You have to go through the whole process : no one will digest a subject for you neatly in advance. If you resort to predigested matter (e.g. the potted literary criticism of manuals), nobody will be pleased and you will be the loser. These short cuts prevent you developing your powers of observation and judgement—which you will need, and which are a more important product of education, even, than knowledge and understanding of a subject.

Take this warning seriously, for if you have come up with wrong ideas on this point it may be some time before you find out, the hard way.

At the University you can make far more mistakes than at school before you are pulled up ; tests are fewer, classes are often larger and held less often. For weeks at a time you may not know how well you are doing, except by your prose-marks. Much of your instruction will probably be in lectures, where the seed is simply sown, to grow if it can. A lecturer will always answer a question after his hour is up, if asked ; but he may never discover it if you are completely at sea. He is in any case not a crammer, not even a sixth-form teacher on your side against the future examiner—he probably is the future examiner. And the degree you hope to get is meant to certify, not only that you absorbed a certain amount of knowledge, but that you mastered the technique of absorbing it. At the stage you have reached nobody, properly speaking, can ' teach ' you any more. The ' teaching staff ' will try to stimulate you to learn and guide you in what to learn; but learning is a thing no one can do for you. They will probably not have time to show you how to learn : that is the purpose of this book.[1]

[1] On the way to organize your work and your time, and the right attitude to acquire, Bruce Truscott, *First Year at the University* (London, Faber, 1946) has some good advice. In the pages that follow I overlap him a little.

TECHNIQUES OF TEACHING AND LEARNING

1. LECTURES

To start, as you will probably start, with the lecture. Its purpose is not to give you the facts you are to learn. To ' cover the course ' is your job; the lecturer's is to use his limited time in the ways he thinks most helpful to you. He may go outside the limits of the syllabus : such excursions may stretch your mind far more than the utilitarian treadmill—and nothing shows up so clearly in examinations as narrowness of interests. He will do his best to smooth out the real difficulties of the subject, try to stimulate your reactions by revealing something of his own, try to illustrate the methods you should follow; but he may very well leave you to do some of the work unaided.

A lecture has two uses—to work on your mind as you listen, and to supply ideas or information you will need to digest later. These last, of course, should be taken down, but often the rest need not. To avoid scribbling useless notes, you need faculties of analysis and discrimination you may not have had occasion to develop till now. A lecture should be listened to critically, never passively. (But this applies to all your work.)

Lecture Notes

First a practical point—you buy your own stationery, and you will do better to buy, not notebooks, but blocks or loose sheets of paper. Carry notes, exercises and everything in one sturdy book-file; then at your leisure sort them into folders (brown paper is good enough), grouping together all your material on one subject, whether lecture-notes, reading-notes or essays. It saves money to buy your paper in bulk; the cheapest on which you can write easily will do, but choose and stick to one size which you can always be sure of obtaining (quarto or foolscap), otherwise storage becomes awkward. It is best to write on one side of the page only, but in any case never fail to start a new page—and a new sheet—for any new subject or section which later you may conceivably want to separate in sorting.

What should your notes look like ?

A very common mistake is to try to take down everything,

and what is more to take it down in complete sentences. You cannot keep pace; you keep falling behind. As a result you neither reproduce the lecture nor listen to it properly—your attention is too divided. Your notes will be full of gaps (which are probably not even marked), and quite useless for revision, because disconnected facts are practically unlearnable. What gives them sense, the ' thread ', is the one thing certain to get lost.

In any case no good classroom lecture would be worth taking down verbatim, for every skilled lecturer ' pads '. The human attention cannot stand more than a certain strain; only a certain number of important notions can be packed successfully into fifty minutes—and they are not too many to be recorded without shorthand by anyone with a fair technique. The first thing is to distinguish which they are, to get the gist—and the lecturer is doing his best to show you. Nothing prevents you adding the odd turn of phrase that takes your fancy or seems to illuminate a point, if you have time.

Bear in mind two principles :

(1) Save time in writing : use initials for names that keep recurring, abbreviate words, omit unnecessary parts of speech, condense statements—only be sure your telegraphese will be clear to you afterwards. Develop your own set of symbols (e.g. // similarly to,)(unlike, → leads to, etc.).

(2) Save labour in rereading—for your notes are made to be used and recopying is usually a waste of time. Certainly you have no time to make indexes, so all notes that fill every line from margin to margin like an essay are condemned in advance : to find anything you want there you may have to read the whole thing. The notes themselves must be their own titles and sub-titles, laid out to catch the eye. Underlining helps, but best of all are titles jutting out into blank space (towards the left, naturally, which is where you begin writing and reading). The matter coming under a title is quite generously ' indented ' (moved over to the right with an imaginary left margin of its own), each new statement on a new line. Never hesitate to ' waste ' paper if it saves trouble later. Titles of subsections jut out, clear of the mass of text but less far to the left than the main titles: titles of lesser divisions, less far again.

With such notes, when you are searching for some detail, you can let your eye travel down the left margin, picking up the main titles until it comes to the one that should contain what you want ; then inwards to the subtitles, and so on. When you are doing a general revision, you can see the plan and the 'thread'—provided only you saw them when you wrote the notes.[1]

You can study an example of this lay-out in G. Lanson, *Esquisse d'une histoire de la tragédie française* (Paris, 1927)—but fortified with 1), 2), 3), (*a*), (*b*), (*c*), which for one's own work should be unnecessary. There is no more efficient method if you can train yourself to analyse and arrange as you follow—and to do so *helps* your understanding of what is being said. I must add that few of my colleagues seem to be so methodical. Everyone must consult his own temperament and find his own solution.

As a specimen, here is this section in note form. As its style was rather condensed, the notes are longer in proportion than they would be for a lecture.

Lecture notes

On loose sheets	One file for all papers
	Sort into folders later by subject
	Buy in bulk, cheap
	Choose 1 size } for
	New sheet / sectn. } sorting

Not verbatim or complete sents.

	Result incoherent & useless
	All lects. *pad*
	Get gist (& odd phrases ?)
Save time writing	Initials
	Abbrev. wds. & sents.
	Condense
	—so long as clear
	Symbols — //)(→
,, ,, rereadg.	
	(Don't recopy)
	,, fill lines
	— imposs. find a detail

[1] You will find more comments on the ' thread ' on p. 53, under *Explication* '.

                    Underline
    (best)   *Layout*—title, subtit. &c.
              Indent progr. → R
              Eye follows L marg. to find pt.
              Plan clear
              cf. Lanson, Esquisse d'ı hist. de la
                  trag. fr.
              (Not in gen. use
              Find own soln.)

2. TUTORIALS

    The 'tutorial' instruction given in most Universities comes
somewhere between the 'tutorial' proper (still found at Oxford
and Cambridge, where they have the manpower), which is a
weekly discussion between a tutor and one student over an
essay, and the 'seminar' (used for advanced work), where
members of a group take turns to read up a question and give a
paper, with a director of studies to act as producer and chair-
man.

    The essence of a good tutorial group is that the tutor is not
there to teach, but to coax ideas out of each member, in discussion (usually) of some piece of work that one of them has
read—letting them, if they will, ask questions, contradict one
another, and spin their own theories. Nothing is so useful for
clearing the mind, showing up absurdities and fallacies, and
driving home and co-ordinating facts picked up in other work.

    Unlike the lecture, the tutorial is your show; and—this fact
is little realised—its failure or success depends on you and your
companions. You do not have to worry too much about talking
foolishly or off the point—the tutor is there to keep the discussion
on the rails. The worst fault you can show is shyness or laziness,
by sitting dumb and cutting yourself off from the whole process
—perhaps ruining it. Because of this fault few groups achieve
what they ought to : students tend to act as if they were still in
a lecture, taking down the tutor's lightest word, speaking only
when directly called on (if then), and paying no attention to their
fellows. It does not occur to them that the student reading the
paper, and even those debating it, are taking the tutor's place

and saying what he intended should be said : he will have to say it if nobody else does, or correct it if it is falsely stated. But if it can arise, with a little stimulus, from a student's own mind, or from the group thinking together, it is all the more likely to stick —' we only know what we have found out for ourselves '. The usefulness of tutorial work to you depends on the degree of your participation.

I should add that there may be even more value in discussion pursued outside the tutor's room, though the style may be different. You may hesitate to talk ' shop ' out of hours; but if you are unable to get excited over at least a few of the problems that turn up, what are you there for ? If the subject does not interest you enough to talk about it, why choose it ?

The well-known definition of a University as a *society* for the pursuit and advancement of learning can only be true for you in so far as you, and your fellows, are willing to make it so.

In modern Universities classes are compulsory because there is no other proof of your attendance. In residential Universities the habitual phrase is that you ' go up to *read* for a degree ', and it is understood that the other forms of instruction, though you would get into trouble if you cut them out entirely, are only adjuncts to reading.

Not every undergraduate lives up to this ideal, needless to say ; and it is harder for many in modern Universities because of daily travel to and from home, lack of quiet at home, and the necessity of finding work in the vacations.[1] But scholarship can only come this way—by treating reading as your principal occupation, one requiring more effort and more reflection than all your essays and exercises, and demanding several hours of several days each week, for at least ten-and-a-half months in the year. The scientist does long hours of ' practicals ' in his laboratory, and writes up his results : our lab. is the library.

On what to read, and how to read, I shall offer some suggestions later.

[1] Vacation work, if it is not a necessity, is a dishonest practice : the public, or your family, is paying for you to be a full-time student for a certain number of years, not in term-time only; courses are not intended to be successfully taken without vacation study.

THE BRANCHES OF FRENCH STUDIES

1. THE STUDY OF LANGUAGE

The study you will be called upon to give to the French language has two main objects—to enable you to read it, not only without errors, but with full appreciation, and to enable you to write it correctly and naturally, with as wide a range as possible of expression and tone. There is a third object, equally important to the Honours student (but normally to him alone), which comes to the fore in ' philological ' and ' linguistic ' work to which we shall come later : it is to investigate, for its own scientific and human interest, the very complex activity of speech.

To confine ourselves here to the first two, writing French has not only its own value as a skill and a mental discipline, but it contributes to reading—you try to make your proses euphonious and rhythmical, not only because there is a prose in the examination, but also to be able to enjoy Chateaubriand and Flaubert.

Conversely, reading is indispensable for writing. To possess a language is to possess a fund of turns of speech so firmly fixed in the memory that they come up without effort when required. They offer us a vast number of patterns, and in each pattern most of the individual words can be replaced by others—so that, even to say something extremely original, we can take and adapt habitual forms of speech. To have a sense of style is to be able to call up, not one, but several suitable patterns, and choose the most appropriate and effective in the circumstances.[1]

This is what we mean by knowing our own language ; a foreign language will never be quite so automatic, but the more the effort the worse the result. Which means that the memory must be fed : ' exercises ' are of little use unless you keep

[1] An interesting and useful attempt at a kind of inventory on these lines is made by H. J. G. Godin, *Les ressources stylistiques du français contemporain*. See *Bibliography*, p. 105, for full details of all books recommended in these pages.

feeding it heavily with new material, for a language is an immense thing. Even our own we never know completely.

If you wish to write well then, you must read a lot. This may not be the most important reason for reading, but it is a vital one for you. You must soak yourself in French and get ' the feel of the language ' as quickly as possible. This means both extensive and intensive reading. It is not enough to restrict yourself to the prescribed text : there should always be one book that you are reading simply for the pleasure of reading and of reading French. Novels are best, or travel books. Read quickly : look up only those words or phrases which seem to be vital or keep recurring, for the aim is fluent reading which will lead you to an almost ' instinctive ' feeling for what is and what is not French. With a little practice you will soon be able to read at least one book a week. But that is only half the matter : you should also do some regular *intensive* reading, with pen, note-book and dictionary at your side. This is inevitably, at first, a fairly slow business, but your vocabulary must be enlarged —especially in certain directions. Many—or most—of your set texts have a restricted, largely abstract vocabulary. The result of this is that very many students are lacking in the words for the concrete objects of present-day life[1]—as they soon discover when they go to France. You must make good any such deficiency. Again novels are the best things to go for : especially those of Balzac, Flaubert, Maupassant, Zola, and more modern writers ranging from Jules Romains and Duhamel to Simenon. And, of course, you will read French newspapers, remembering, however, that the modernisms you find in them and enter in your phrase-book are not to be used in your own writing except with the very greatest care.

The phrase-book (carried with you, or written up at leisure from the backs of envelopes) should be a valuable and valued aid. Enter in it (1) every word you have met and didn't know (unless it is so technical that the chances are you will never see it again),

[1] The late Professor Ritchie made this point, quoting his own notes : ' Large First Year Honours class : 30 bright people; nobody knew the French for ' poker ', ' starch ', ' switch ' or ' tea-pot '—perhaps not high-class enough to be found in any of the Set Texts '. *Modern Languages*, vol. XXXV, no. 2, March, 1954, p. 45.

and (2) every word you knew occurring in a phrase you didn't know. Enter with it a translation, and be sure the translation is exact. Note—if you know or can find out—the ' flavour ' of the word or phrase (uneducated, or slangy, or for literary use only, or poetical, or archaic). Enter the whole phrase, stripped only of inessential additions, as a dictionary would; rarely, for technical terms, you can enter a word by itself because the phrase would not help—but at least, with nouns, add an article or an adjective to enable you to learn the gender. It is better to have an order, marked in your book in advance : simple alphabetical order (for the key-words of each phrase) is probably the best. Write the English on the opposite page, to facilitate revision. Your words and phrases will come, not only from private reading, but from prose and translation classes and even lectures on set books.

You cannot do without your own dictionary—not a pocket dictionary compiled for tourists, and not a medium-sized, medium-priced one like Gasc or Cassell, which will only confuse you with its masses of unexplained renderings for the difficult words.[1] If you are an Honours student you should possess the big Mansion French-English dictionary published by Harrap (I am not speaking here of English-French dictionaries, which are purely utilitarian aids for writing exercises), and the *Petit Larousse*, invaluable for its concise definitions (usually more informative than renderings) and its illustrations; or at the very least the shorter Mansion or the *Concise Oxford* (by Chevalley). You should know, and consider buying, the *Dictionnaire des synonymes* and *Dictionnaire analogique* (published by Larousse), which suggest, and discriminate between, different renderings of the same idea, or nearly related ideas, among which may be the word you need for your prose, or the exact nuance to express your thought in a dissertation.

You must depend on your library for the four learned volumes of Littré, with its abundant quotations from classical authors, the

[1] Look up, e.g., the word *coup*, which has several different but related senses (knock, noise of a blow, movement of a blow, one of several movements or occasions). Gasc and Cassell give dozens of one-word renderings followed by a few phrases. Mansion, Littré and Robert sort out the senses, arrange them under definitions, and illustrate each by complete phrases.

shorter but more recent *Dictionnaire Général* of Hatzfeld and Darmsteter and the so-called 'nouveau Littré', now being brought out by P. Robert, which, with its modern quotations and cross-references to synonyms and antonyms, will be even more useful to you. It is in the library, surrounded by these, that you should work on your proses; you should compile lists of difficulties to bring to them, search them at leisure, under all the likely words, for the expression which escapes you, and read whole articles to discover the richness and flexibility of the commonest words, the ones you thought you knew.

With the dictionary must be mentioned the grammar. For reading, you should rarely or never want it (parts of irregular verbs are given in their alphabetical place by Mansion; genders, plurals and a lot of constructions can be found under the appropriate word), but you ought to use it often, and develop a conscience about using it, for composition. It matters a good deal what grammar. If the one you got used to at school is really complete (not simplified) and laid out in order (not in doses of graded difficulty separated by other matter), stick to it. If not, I recommend J. E. Mansion, *A Grammar of Present-day French*, which is full of illustrated sentences. So was R. L. G. Ritchie, *Nelson's French Grammar* and *Nelson's Third French Course* (the same text with useful exercises): but both are unfortunately out of print. When one of these has been mastered——as it should be before you come up to the university, or at the *very latest* by the first year of your course—Grevisse, *Le bon usage*, will introduce you to the really interesting stage where grammar shades into stylistics. This book, together with Brunot's *La pensée et la langue* and Bally's *Traité de stylistique*, is essential reading for the Honours student.

For some this attention to rules, some of them illogical, some affecting only a single letter or sound, is, it must be admitted, irritating or uncongenial. It is, however, an indispensable part of the study of ' French language and literature '. For what immediately distinguishes the study of French or German or indeed any language from other kinds of subjects but precisely this, that before all else it is concerned with what the language allows you

16

to do with it, i.e. the means of expression available in it, and the use that has been made of them ? So very important is grammar, that anyone who continues to find it irritating, anyone who does not urgently want to study French as a linguistic discipline, would be well advised to transfer his allegiance to another subject before it is too late. For without strict and accurate attention to language your literary work is bound to be superficial and inaccurate, your writing of French will be unnatural and valueless, if not worse, and your study of philology without point. This last point is most important. Do not keep separate the past history of the language (' philology ') and its present state (' grammar '); they are two aspects of the same thing and you will often find that the history of the language, by explaining the word-forms and sentence structure of modern French, will help you to understand the ' illogicalities ' of grammar already referred to. Quite apart from that, language is perhaps the most important faculty that differentiates man from the beasts, and the study of language, i.e. grammar and philology, is surely therefore worthy of the attention of any intelligent being.

To sum up, the ideal is the readiness born of long familiarity, backed by the accuracy and discrimination that comes of scholarly study.

One warning, and it ought not to be necessary to add this; but so many students come up these days incapable of writing the simplest sentence in correct French, that it must be said. If you are not capable at once, without the slightest hesitation, of giving the past historic of *vivre*, the preposition used after *essayer* or the French for ' he should have come ', then you are not alone, but you will do no good and will be passed by no conscientious examiner till you have worked like a fury, recovered the power to learn accurately by heart that you should have developed at school, and made good an elementary and absolutely damning deficiency. You must do this in your first year, or it will be too late.

Prose Composition

This exercise is always a little artificial in the early stages, and some teachers think it is made too much of : the beginner, who has not read very much real French, and has had little time to acquire a fund of living expressions and get the 'feel' of the language as it should be used, is trying to construct it synthetically with the aid of a grammar and a dictionary. Nevertheless great importance is attached to the prose in all British Universities— partly because it has been taken over from the Latin (and Greek) prose which was the backbone of the traditional classical curriculum; but also because it is a first-rate exercise for developing logical analysis and aesthetic response.

There are two requirements for a perfect prose composition : (1) It should give an exact equivalent of the meaning of the original. This in itself is not so easy (though it is only half the battle). It takes care and intelligence, often, to see the real meaning and discard mistaken first impressions—the exact sense, as shown by the context, of a word or a statement that could have several, the logical progression (even if only implied) from one step to the next, must first be grasped before they can be rendered. It is surprising how often students fail here. And, since none of us knows his own language perfectly, an English dictionary must be part of your equipment as well as a French one (preferably the *Concise Oxford* as a constant stand-by and the *O.E.D.* in the library for the more obstinate problems). It will be a good thing if you get one or two pieces of archaic or poetic English to translate each year, just to drive home the need of knowing what every word and expression really means.

I have given some advice about the use of a dictionary. There are other points to bear in mind when you are using it for translation into French. No need to dwell on crass mistakes like using the translation of a homonym (a word with the same form but entirely different meaning) like *cor* for 'corn' (grain), *brûlure* for 'burn' (brook)—nor on well-known *faux amis du traducteur* like *supporter*, which does not mean 'support'. It is just as bad to neglect the grammatical indications in your dictionary, e.g. to take a verb marked *v.n.* (or *v.i.*) and give it a direct object.

You must fix in your mind the fact that French words are not equivalents of English words—languages are not codes. Even the simple material things called chairs and tables are not always called *chaises* and *tables*. But for more complicated notions—

18

especially dealing with abstract concepts—the only safe course is to say ' This English word stands—in this context—for some idea or reality which I must define; when I have got the definition I should be able to find the French word that fits it '. You are not translating words, but meanings. Any given word, French or English, covers not one notion but a group of closely-related notions, an *area* of meaning not always clearly charted; and the area covered by an English word is hardly ever exactly the same as that covered by the nearest French word. The two may have similar forms and a common origin; but national ways of life and thought have been at work on them, drawing them in different directions. ' Renown ', ' glory ', ' honour ', ' esteem ', ' reputation ', ' prestige ', occupy neighbouring and overlapping territories, and correspond very often to their opposite numbers in the French series *renom, gloire, honneur, estime, réputation, prestige* : but *gloire* shades off into ' vainglory ' on the one side, and (in 17th-century writers) into ' honour ' or ' reputation ' on the other; Shakespeare's use of ' reputation ' is sometimes *honneur* ; the French *prestige* has far wider meanings than the recent English borrowing. Again, the second and third in each series can be extended to mean ' *cause of* high esteem ' (' the glories of French art '), the others cannot. Then what about ' fame ', ' repute ', *renommée*, which have no opposite numbers ? And this is a relatively simple example.

One practical counsel arises from all this : that it is never enough to copy a word from an English-French dictionary— unless you find a phrase which testifies that the word is in common use in the sense you want. The phrases in dictionaries are more valuable to you than anything else there; for words live in groups, not singly. (*Avis* means ' opinion ' (sometimes !); you must know when, and also know *à mon avis*, but DE *l'avis de tout le monde*). The English-French dictionary has its uses, for there are words that slip the memory, and words one has never known; but the bulk of your work when writing a prose should be done on the French-English dictionary (with phrases) or, better, on a French-French, with phrases and also definitions : the *Petit Larousse* for quick reference, the big Littré or Robert for careful checking.

I have already said you can learn a lot of French in them. Every word found in an English-French dictionary, unless certified by a phrase, must then be checked in this way.

But some words are ' untranslatable ' : ' quaint ', ' homely ', ' fun ', have no exact French equivalent in any context. Other words than these, when you look them up in the English-French Mansion, you will find rendered by words you will very likely realize to be unsuitable in the context you have to translate. But if you stop to ask yourself what meaning they contribute, in the passage you are working on, that meaning can always be conveyed, somehow or other—perhaps by re-wording, and using a verb when the original word was a noun, or an adverbial phrase instead of an adjective, or two words instead of one. All these devices are legitimate *if necessary*. There is always more re-wording to do for a perfect translation than the beginner realises, but it must not be done wantonly.

(2) The other half of the battle, the other ideal requirement, is that the translation should have, for a Frenchman, exactly the same flavour as the original has for us. There are several points to consider. Words and expressions may be, at one extreme, slangy, or at the other, suitable only for poetry or the most solemn occasions—there is a whole scale of gradations between, and you have to judge the place occupied by the English expression, then by the French you intend to replace it with. (The fund of every-day expressions you bring back after a stay in France, or which you can get from conversation classes, is of the greatest value, but is subject to this danger; for good informal spoken French is not always acceptable as written French. The notes *Pop.*, *Fam.*, *Vulg.*, in dictionaries are only too commonly ignored.) Again, they may have been chosen for some quality of their sounds— you have to perceive this and try to find equivalents, or at least avoid accidental jingles, too-prominent alliterations and other uglinesses to which the French ear is very sensitive. Finally the passage is almost certain to have a rhythm of some kind—agitated (full of stresses and pauses), or terse and emphatic, or flowing and easy, or majestic and periodic; this too should be reproduced as far as French—and your French—allows.

The only way to come anywhere near success is to have the cadences of French prose, of a similar style and flavour, ' ringing in your ears ' as you write; for this reason, before you start, read over, aloud or half-aloud, a page of the most nearly similar French you can find—choose it if you like from some collection of prose extracts in your syllabus which you know fairly well, and choose only modern writers and writers you know to be good. And, of course, re-read your prose aloud when you think it is finished.

You will have grasped that these two requirements—exact sense and exact flavour—are often quite irreconcilable : the only rendering that fulfils the first turns out to violate the second. As always in such dilemmas, the only solution is to compromise as cleverly as you can. But you will understand why a good prose can only result from a rough copy full of rejected alternatives. One of the beginner's mistakes is to stick to his first draft without doubts or hesitations.

However, the prose is not merely an exercise for the ingenuity and knowledge you already possess; it should enrich your phrase-book and your memory. It is little use to transcribe words and phrases from the dictionary into your copy if they do not come to rest in your mind. You will have no dictionary to use, well or badly, in the examination; and though your performance then is bound to be less perfect, it rests with you to ensure in advance that the collapse is not complete. An excellent suggestion[1] is to take your weekly prose in three stages :

(1) A preliminary exploration, ending in a first draft, without any aids. Find out how much of the text you can translate straight off, but, more important, discover the gaps in your knowledge; then find makeshifts such as you would have to use in an examination—fully conscious that they are makeshifts, but trying to be quite sure that they are genuine French and not English in fancy spelling. In some cases you will be beaten (as, always, for concrete nouns); in others you will find periphrases, more or less clumsy. This needs, and also develops, critical linguistic sense. To make the most of this faculty, and to discover your own shortcomings, is the purpose of this stage.

[1] For which we are indebted to Mr. J. Killa Williams, M.A., lecturer in French in the University College of Wales, Aberystwyth.

(2) The ' research ' or dictionary stage. Use the best dictionaries, in the way described, watching all the indications, reading whole articles, following up cross-references; then copy all you have discovered into the phrase-book; then, consciously and deliberately, *learn* the new material. Do the same for grammatical difficulties : plug the gaps you have revealed in your knowledge, and consciously and deliberately *learn* the new material.

(3) The final state to be handed in. Write it with all aids put out of sight—dictionaries, grammars, phrase-book, draft and any other notes—, testing the knowledge that has come to rest in your mind, under self-imposed examination conditions.

In this way alone can you be sure that your French is your own possession, and really at your disposal whenever you want it, in examinations or in real life.

Excellent advice, both fuller and more technical, can be found in the introductions to Berthon and Onions, *Advanced French Composition*, Ritchie and Moore, *A Manual of French Composition*, and R. L. G. Ritchie, *A New Manual of French Composition*, and especially in the model lessons of the last two.

Students sometimes ask how one can improve one's proses by private work. Firstly, by study of one's corrected work and the fair copy—but only provided that it has been taken down accurately : it is surprising how often students mis-copy the correction or improvement they have been given; the harm that can be done is obvious. Master, if you can, the meaning of the symbols used in correcting : some teachers simply underline what is unsuitable and cross through what is downright wrong. Professor Ritchie's first manual explains his notation, which some of his many former colleagues and pupils may still imitate —dotted underline for poor phrasing, wavy underline for poor choice of word, straight double underline for doubtful tense (accompanied in each case by a cross-stroke, for an absolute mistake of the same type). The French write notes in the margin :

fs	faux sens	mistranslation, wrong meaning
cs	contresens	mistranslation making the author say the opposite of what he means
barb	barbarisme	word that does not exist

imp	impropre	word that cannot be used in this sense, or context, or construction
sol	solécisme	construction that does not exist
inc	incorrect	construction breaking a major rule of grammar
in	inexact	minor grammatical error
m.d.	mal dit	'not French' though not a grammatical error
angl	anglicisme	wrong, or non-existent, word or construction modelled on an English one
acc	accord	(wrong) agreement
t	temps	(wrong) tense

TB, B, AB très bien, bien, assez bien

Secondly (need I say ?), by re-reading one's grammar and learning the grammatical forms and the rules.

Thirdly, by increasing one's fund of French—learn the illustrative sentences in the grammar, especially if they are genuine quotations from authors : revise the sentences in your own phrase-book; learn French passages, of the type I advised you to read as models—but not your fair copies, which, however good, are not authentic original French.

Fourthly, by the useful exercise of translating a passage from French into the best and most natural English you can, putting it aside for a day or two, then translating back and comparing. You will not recapture the idiomatic and stylistic turns of the original, but you may learn them by the process of trying. But the translation must be very careful and accurate in the first place, or you will only be driving false notions into your head. You can also try translating back from published English translations of French works; but in most cases you will lay bare so many faults in the printed English that you will learn—what is perhaps worth learning—how very shoddy most pieces of commercial translation are.

Translation from French

It is to be hoped that you will have fairly frequent written exercises in translation, and not always ' unseen '. It is as important, as difficult, and as instructive as translation the other way.[1] The principles are exactly the same. The aim—to produce

[1] For good advice on this, and other points, see J. G. Weightman, *On Language and Translation*.

23

English which, while faithful, is as good in all respects as the French—ought to be more nearly within your reach; but only if your command of English is sure, your range wide, your standards and taste good—only, in other words, if you read good English habitually and with the same critical sense you try to bring to French.

The Dissertation

Original composition in French, since it may equally well have a general or a literary subject, can best be described here.

The most elementary form of ' free composition ' needs no rules : its aim is to see if you can say something for yourself in French, and it is implicitly understood that nobody minds much what you say. The ' essay ' done for a tutor (in French or English), embodying the results of a piece of study—what is called in France an *exposé*—needs only to be clear, methodical and businesslike; though to attain these simple ends the rules of the dissertation help greatly.

The ' English essay ' treated as an end in itself, on the other hand, has been influenced, as its name implies, by the example of wayward talents like that of Lamb; it tends to be an exercise in self-expression, aiming to interest and impress by a display of imagination and ' personality '. As against this, the French *dissertation* is a training in disciplined thought and applied logic —very difficult to pick up for the British student trained in opposite methods, and all the more valuable for that.

What the two have in common is that, to treat a serious subject suitably, the writer has to draw on all his knowledge and all his ideas—not connected with French only, but gathered from his other studies, from private reading, from newspapers, from conversation. Any type of essay is a test of intelligence, taste and general culture.

Perhaps I should pause to answer here the question once asked by a freshman who had brought in a transcription from an encyclopedia : ' Do you mean we have to write what we think ? ' —Yes and no. What you have thought up to now about the subject may not amount to much. Get the relevant facts, master them, think hard about them, then write what you think.

24

The *dissertation*, in this country, is still usually called the ' French essay ', but most, perhaps all, Universities have tried to adopt the standards imposed in France : it is a pity the English name is kept. However, a composition obeying the rules of the *dissertation* cannot fail to be acceptable as an ' essay ', while the reverse is not true.

Whimsy is here at a discount. Failure to see the point, and wandering from the point, are crimes. In what I consider its highest form, the dissertation gives you a problem to solve, or a statement to prove or refute, by cogent reasoning or pertinent illustrations. There is a lower form, looking very much like a typical ' essay ', which calls, or seems to call, for nothing but description or careful laying-out of facts. Such is the subject often met with in elementary examinations, on the uses of travel or reading or leisure; or, in literary papers, the (very dull) kind of question that begins ' Montrez que . . . ' Sometimes with these nothing more can be done than to lay out the fairly obvious relevant considerations in the most efficient order, find some objections and dutifully refute them, and end with a Q.E.D.

But often a doubt or an objection introduced to be removed only at the last moment will transform the dull-seeming subject into the more interesting kind—an enquiry or a debate. Always try to find this twist; it is sufficient usually to take the objection first : ' Is it true that . . . (A) ? Does it not seem, on the contrary, that . . . (B) ? For consider that . . . (1), . . . (2), . . . (3), etc. However, it can be answered that . . . (1), . . . (2), etc. Therefore proposition (B) is demolished and we must conclude after all that . . . (A).'

This is the ' dramatic ' method of presentation, in the sense in which a play is ' dramatic ' when you are not allowed to see how the situation will work out until the final scene. It arouses interest by the simplest and strongest means—curiosity, suspense. It may seem childish to talk of arousing suspense in an examiner who understands the question better than you do and has been reading a whole bundle of fairly similar answers : it is not. An important element in the art of writing is the art of inducing the reader to read on; it is one you cannot afford to neglect. Even the

25

examiner is not indifferent to the pleasure of having his curiosity tickled and finally rewarded. Only, as in drama, without careful planning you produce not suspense but bewilderment. On clarity of plan, see later, p. 31.

The question you treat must be a real one, legitimately arising from the subject set. In the more interesting type of subject (e.g. a quotation from a philosopher or critic) the difficulty is often not to find a question (it is full of questions) but to find the right one—to see, under the epigrammatic or figurative or allusive form of expression, what is the statement which is being made, and which you are called upon to formulate more sharply and then challenge, test, and prove or correct.

When you are not in the examination room, it is wise to look up the context if you can, to make sure of the author's drift, the meaning he attaches to his terms, and his line of argument. (All this you may, and sometimes must, bring into your discussion.) If you cannot do this, you must subject the quotation to a severe analysis and *explication* (see later) for your own benefit. To make it say what it does not say is the most serious of errors : it throws your whole *dissertation* on the wrong track. Avoid at all costs, if there is any alternative, an epigram you do not understand.

Once you have understood the subject, what are you going to do with it ?—I am speaking still of your initial reflection, preceding the writing and even the planning of your *dissertation*. The obvious first question is : Is it true ? Try to put up alternative statements; see if they can be maintained. Then see what are the presuppositions on which it rests : often the discussion should bear on these. For example: ' Tout amusement inutile est un mal pour un être dont la vie est si courte et le temps si précieux ' (J.-J. Rousseau). To assume this as true and go on to list legitimate and illegitimate activities, is to miss all the possibilities of the subject, which lie in testing the two or three propositions taken blandly for granted. ' Life is short '. ' There is much to do.' What ? Why ? ' Mere self-indulgence is harmful.' But are there *amusements utiles ?* There is a subject which is not entirely platitude.[1]

Or it may be the consequences of the statement that appear

[1] See specimen plans, Appendix A (1).

most interesting (what follows if it is true ?). But if they conflict violently with accepted notions, then once again there is something in the premisses to examine. Take another example : ' L'histoire est du roman qui a été ; le roman est de l'histoire qui aurait pu être.' Not universally true, obviously : some kinds of history have nothing in common with most kinds of novel. The quotation implies that there is one ' right ' kind of novel, which, except for being fictitious, has methods and aims like those of (one kind of) history. In fact, the Goncourt brothers, who wrote this, believed in the sociological novel documented from observed cases; their name at the foot of the quotation should have recalled this to you, or led you to discover it; after which your task is much easier. Define first (since it is not the heart of the matter) the kind of social history which serves as comparison, then describe this ideal of the novel in more detail (in the abstract ; in concrete examples). Are there drawbacks or dangers ? Do you wish to propose a different type or types as better or equally valid (with examples)? Argue for them in the same way. Conclude for or against the Goncourts, or with reservations.

This example brings out another point. A *dissertation littéraire* such as the above involves knowledge you can supply from your literature studies (and, in this way, may be safer ground than philosophical questions on the duties and rights of the individual, the nature of liberty, and so on); but you must not write it as you would an essay or examination answer in a literature course (where the quotation would probably be followed by the instructions ' Discuss with reference to . . . ' some set book). There, you would analyse the meaning of the statement, say what you know of the sources of the ideas expressed and the author's reasons for holding them, and compare his practice with his preaching. In a *dissertation*, the first point is just as important, the next two may be relevant (probably in your introduction) and the third scarcely relevant, to be dismissed in a paragraph; but the main discussion must be on the *general* truth of the statement. Discussion of Molière's dictum, ' L'emploi de la comédie est de corriger les vices des hommes ', does not end with *Tartuffe* or with the whole of Molière's comedies, but embraces the nature and function of Comedy everywhere.

The search for the matter of what you are going to write is not ended before you think you have enough strong arguments and suitable examples or illustrations to prove the proposition you are going to support, and—this must not be omitted, if your treatment is to be at all complete—the best available arguments and examples for possible alternative propositions which you will look at and reject.

I said that the *dissertation* is an exercise in logic. It is not necessary to have studied formal logic, for the same methods of demonstration were used in the algebra and geometry you did at school : it is necessary to be able to see when an argument is faulty, what presuppositions are implied by a statement, and how much support is really given by a fact, an example or a quotation you adduce—whether it clinches the matter; or supports, but not conclusively; or simply clarifies by substituting something concrete for an abstraction. To be able to use these examples, and to know their worth, is an art of the greatest importance—no unsupported statement of yours has any interest to anyone; you are not asked to say what you think, but why everyone should think so too.

Be as original as you can—in the right sense, of trying to think for yourself, and not being content with dreary commonplaces; but not in the bad sense of forsaking common sense for flashy paradoxes. They will not impress.

When you have assembled your matter (in rough jottings) it is time to consider the order and form it should be given. What should be clear is that the order in which points came into your head will not do; yet many students never realize this, and produce what may be called effusions or even, by courtesy, essays, but not *dissertations*. The best advice is still that of the King of Hearts : ' Begin at the beginning and go on till you come to the end : then stop.' There must be an introduction and a conclusion, particularly a conclusion—the conclusion is the section without which the whole is obviously incomplete, and after which there is obviously no more to say; the introduction announces the questions to which the answer is only given in the conclusion. And yet introduction and conclusion are the sections most commonly neglected or omitted. It is not always easy to see what should go into each. ' La dernière chose qu'on trouve en faisant un ouvrage est de savoir celle qu'il faut mettre la première.' (This was said by Pascal, the same writer who once apologised for not having had time to make his composition shorter). It is true that the best moment to say what you are going to do is after you have done it. (You can, and should, do this in an exercise, by drafting the Introduction last; but in an examination you will not have time for so much recopying, and will have to rely on a careful plan.) The worst mistake, and the commonest, is to put the conclusion in the first lines of the Introduction—by at once answering yes or no to the question which forms the subject. It is a natural thing to do : you have been asked something, so you make your answer clear without waste of time—but (1) it is undramatic : you have given away all hope of surprise; (2) it puts you in the position of making statements before proving them, instead of after; and (3) what have you left for your conclusion, except to repeat the same formula once more?

In planning the middle section, the first aim is to lead from your starting-point to your conclusion by steps which are clear and compel assent, just as in mathematics or logic. The second (for the first does not eliminate all alternatives) is to create as much interest as possible by using opportunities for climax or contrast; the third, to avoid repetition as much as you can without straining the reader's memory.

Even the barest subjects allow choice of plan. Take a simple ' Montrez que . . . ' question involving a set author : you will obviously collect and display facts and examples either supporting the statement or (seemingly at least) at variance with it, then discuss and strike a balance. But you may either take your examples one by one (in what order ? it is up to you) and mark up points *pro* and *con.* as you go, or you may build up two big groups (each in the order you please)—examples *pro* and examples *con.* (or better, *con.* first, to produce suspense). If each example is going to require the same sort of discussion, the grouped order will save repetition. On the other hand, to take points in the order of the story, or the chronological order of the books, may give a clearer idea of the writer's work.

But, by whatever route, the plan must move from the problem to its solution, or from the proposition to the Q.E.D. Every step necessary for this must be included, everything else must be omitted. Be ruthless with irrelevancies, or the examiner will.

In one sense, no plan is compulsory. No two people will treat the same subject in exactly the same way. But many of the components can, in the nature of things, hardly ever be omitted or displaced. Here then is the layout which will nearly always be necessary.

The *Introduction* may have to contain up to four sections :

1 (optional). The *entrée en matière* which aims, as it were, to invite the reader to come inside the defined and limited subject you are to treat. Like the orator's ' exordium ' in classical Rhetoric, it tries to put him on your side—i.e. to show why it should interest him to read on. It should be no more than a sentence or two; there is no time or space to waste. It can be omitted, but to come straight to business looks a little bare.

2 Before you can state how you understand the subject, you must define any terms that need defining. If you neglect this —especially for terms of criticism like ' classical ', ' romantic ', ' realist ', some of which are extremely vague and various in meaning, but also for words like ' roman ' and ' histoire ' in the example discussed above—not only do you risk finding that the (unformulated) definition in your mind changes as you go along, so that in the end you are talking about a different concept (and what you said at first does not apply), but even if this does not happen you will not know exactly what it is you have to prove. But there are great dangers, too, in laying down an *arbitrary* definition. If your subject is ' Quel est, à votre avis, le personnage le plus tragique d'*Andromaque ?* ' you *are* expected to choose your own definition of *tragique* (which you must state, before the reader can follow and judge your discussion of the character preferred); if on the other hand a generally-accepted definition is assumed (' Le personnage d'Andromaque est-il tragique ? ') care

is required in finding it, and some reading may be necessary; if, finally, the word to be defined occurs in a quotation (if you have somebody else's statement that ' Le personnage d'Andromaque n'est pas tragique ') it is the author's (implicit) definition that matters, and if you fail to find it you will only be proving, or disproving, a statement he never meant to make. Your own definition may come in as well, as an alternative worthy of discussion. You are free of course to reject his, but first you must know—or guess—what it is, and state it clearly.

There are cases where the definition is a large part of the discussion (e.g. 'Corneille n'a pas le sens du tragique ').. Here it will be better to leave the definition as a problem to be solved in the body of the essay, pointing out in the Introduction what you are doing.[1]

3 When your terms are defined, reformulate the subject as clearly as possible, showing any subsidiary questions it involves. (This is the section that looks forward to the Conclusion, where this question or these questions will be answered in the same terms). Many teachers advise you to make this section, not a question, but a statement of what you intend to prove (like the ' proposition ' of a theorem; the same name is used in the old Rhetorics.) You gain in clarity, but you lose in dramatic suspense. In either form, this is the part of your Introduction that must never be omitted : if the reader does not know what you are trying to do he cannot judge whether you are doing it. For that matter, if you do not put it on record, you are in danger of forgetting yourself.

4 (optional). It is often advantageous at the end of the Introduction to announce the plan of the discussion to follow— explicitly and formally, with a word of explanation for the order chosen, or implicitly, for instance by a string of questions through which you mean to reach the answer to the main question.

You must have an order in any case; a practised writer may avoid stating it in pedantic detail—but it must, stated or unstated, be visible and obvious, from the beginning and at every turn of the discussion; nothing is more infuriating to the reader than not

---

[1] See two possible plans, Appendix A (ii).

to see where he is being led—he suspects a blind alley at once; and it is safer to be too plain than not to be plain enough. A skeleton is more attractive with the flesh and skin on, but the bare bones are better than a shapeless mass. Pay great attention to the skeleton and never hide it too thoroughly; while you are a beginner at least, let the main bones show through.

The *body* or *middle* of the *dissertation* follows and works out the plan, without prolixity and without obscurity.

' Easy reading means damn' hard writing,' and usually much revision. Even when your thought is clear to you, it still has to be made clear to the reader.

Support each statement by proof or example.

Take one point at a time. Descartes' second rule of method was to ' diviser chacune des difficultés que j'examinerais en autant de parcelles qu'il se pourrait, et qu'il serait requis pour les mieux résoudre '.

Give each a paragraph to itself. This is another aspect of letting the reader see where he is going. Whenever possible let the first sentence or phrase of the paragraph announce its subject. If you branch into multiple examples or sub-headings, the last sentence should sum up the paragraph. (When you analyse good authors, watch how they observe this rule. For your kind of work it is very important.)

The *Conclusion* answers the Introduction and states as clearly as possible what you believe you have demonstrated. Only the contributory secondary questions should have their answers stated in the body of the *dissertation*. The principal answer *is* the Conclusion : do not anticipate it or give it twice. Like the dénouement of a classical play, the Conclusion should tie up all the ends and ' then stop '. It must not include afterthoughts, for all ideas, especially all arguments, must find their proper place in the plan or else be cut out; but it may, in a few sentences, lead out of your subject as the *entrée en matière* led into it, and relate your findings to the wider field of thought you started from.

To those who find their French does not stand up well to the strain of divided attention—and they are many; only in your last year can you hope to have a reasonably flexible and correct style at your command—I would say : do not let the limitations of your French reduce you to baby-talk, insist on making it say what you want to say; but do not let your thought lead you into involved constructions where you know you are not safe. The deepest thought can be expressed in the simplest syntax (which is the best, for you especially), if only you work hard enough on it. Break down the complex sentences into several simple ones; take out the parentheses, the qualifications, the reservations, make main clauses of them and find the right position for each. Do this in English first if you must, and on paper if you like. An idea is not tied to the words in which it first occurred to you.

> Ce que l'on conçoit bien s'énonce clairement,
> Et les mots pour le dire arrivent aisément.

It is the half-formed thought, veiled in ambiguous phraseology, that gives the trouble. Think it out before you write it.

Revise your *dissertations* with all the care you give to a prose. It should be unnecessary to say this, but the mind gets so fixed on the matter that it easily becomes blind to the words.

And to the more ambitious stylists, I commend the advice of an Oxford tutor quoted by Dr. Johnson : ' Read over your compositions, and whenever you meet with a passage which you think is particularly fine, strike it out.' Purple patches are often due to haze.

Excellent additional advice on the *dissertation* will be found in Bouvier et Jourda, *Guide de l'étudiant en littérature française.* Professor D. Mornet's booklet, *Comment il faut composer et rédiger une dissertation française* goes deeper, but his discussion of types of plans is addressed to those with a more formal philosophical training than the British student possesses. Collections of model *dissertations littéraires*—e.g. Mornet, *La littérature française enseignée par la dissertation*, and Rayot et Roustan, *La composition littéraire, psychologique* . . .—provide instructive plans to study— so long as they are not used, any more than histories of literature should be used, as sources of knowledge and criticism dispensing with personal acquaintance with texts.

C

Old French

You will almost certainly be expected to study Old French, the language of medieval Northern France. Your aim should be to achieve such a knowledge of the language at that stage in its history as will enable you to (1) translate at sight any passage in Old French and (2) explain the structural peculiarities of the language then written. This you will achieve partly by practice : you will be reading and translating the prescribed medieval texts and will discover or have pointed out to you the features that characterize Old French; you will also, it is to be hoped, read in the same way, either in an anthology or otherwise, passages extracted from texts written at different periods and in different dialects. But such practical contact with the language is not enough : it leads to piecemeal knowledge that needs systematizing. (The constant danger with linguistic work is that the fascination of the isolated fact tempts you to stop at that point and to omit the essential organizing of the material).

To enable you to see Old French as a linguistic system you will therefore probably be offered a separate course of lectures. But it may be that there are no such lectures, but instead courses on the history of the language from Latin to modern French, under various headings : phonology, morphology, syntax.[1] In this case you are expected to abstract the elements proper to Old French and use these when faced with a text or linguistic problem. (This is not an ideal method, but is perhaps made necessary in your French department by a shortage of class-hours : the historical method seems to cover more ground in the time available). This abstracting of the Old French elements is not difficult, but if you find it confusing, then you would be well advised to base your purely medieval work on such a work as Foulet, *Petite syntaxe de l'ancien français*. This excellent and readable book is based on the study of a restricted number of French texts of the 13th century. The author examines the forms found in those works—the noun, the verb, and the invariable words—and the use to which they are put, ending with a section on word-order. He studies many quotations from his

[1] See below, p. 38 ff.

34

texts, and constantly explains the language by reference to the thought-processes of those who were using it. Foulet's point of view is almost exclusively Old French : he does not refer back to Latin origins and only rarely does he bring modern developments into the picture. In this way he keeps you from considering Old French as merely a half-way stage between Latin and present-day French, and you should therefore see it as a language, that, to its users, speakers or writers, seemed as steady and permanent as Modern French or English does to us.

If you view Old French in the way Foulet does, you should proceed on the right lines and avoid the usual errors of students. You will realize that it is for all practical purposes a new foreign language to learn and that this calls for all the normal language-learning techniques that you presumably, as an Honours student, learned so well at school : the keeping of vocabulary and other note-books, the systematic learning of vocabulary, morphology, syntax, etc. But in your study you have the great advantage that you have your knowledge of both modern French and English to help you memorize the Old French. For example, students have more than once told me that such and such a word was not in the appropriate Old French dictionaries and have been surprised to learn that the reason is that the word still survives and is to be found in Mansion. Apart from the *faux amis* that exist here as elsewhere (O.F. *jolif*, *joli*, for example, is different in meaning from Modern French *joli*), your knowledge of present-day French will be very helpful. Further you, as an English-speaking student, have this advantage over your French counterpart : many words came into English from Old French and have retained the older meaning (and much of the older pronunciation) since lost by French. English *jolly* is a case in point, while O.F. *jeu parti* is more easily remembered when you think of *jeopardy* (even if the meanings are not identical). Again such a construction as *je sui chantanz* seems more ' sensible ' when you think of English continuous tenses.

And yet, although you will seek all the help the present-day language affords, you should try to avoid viewing Old French through Modern French eyes. For example, today if a finite verb is not accompanied by a substantival subject, then, except on rare occasions, a personal pronoun subject is expressed; in Old French, however, as you soon discover, a verbal form will often be accompanied by neither substantive nor pronoun as subject. Students often express this by speaking of the ' omission of the personal pronoun '. This is to view the phenomenon from a point of view foreign to the Old French writer : he was following quite a definite speech habit which required the pronoun to be expressed in certain cases, but not in others.[1] This is, by the way, one example of that freedom of construction that often seems to characterize medieval as opposed to modern French. While recognizing this greater freedom of the older language, you should also see that it *is* a linguistic system that has its own, often subtly motivated habits : every possible word order for the main parts of the sentence (subject, verb, object) is found, yet writers do not use any order in any context : the verb has its own place in the structure of the sentence, the type of word which stands first influences the order of those that follow, etc.[2]

You will get a much clearer picture of Old French if you follow Foulet in keeping to a norm to which deviant forms can be referred. If, for example, you take as your norm Francien (the language spoken in the Ile de France) in the 12th or 13th centuries, then you can learn the pronunciation, morphology, etc. to be found in texts written by natives of that area. Then, when you meet a text of an earlier or later date (and remember that the period covered by your reading stretches over as much time as from the Renaissance to to-day), you can note the linguistic differences. Similarly, you will read passages in other dialects than Francien, and the dialectal differences will be more clearly evident if you have a norm against which to set them. The dialects give students a fair amount of trouble, so that you should acquaint yourself with the list of dialectal peculiarities given in Pope's *From Latin to Modern French*, pages 486–505. This will save you much unnecessary searching of the dictionary[3] for

[1] Cf. W. von Wartburg, *Problèmes et méthodes de la linguistique*, pp. 50–63.

[2] Cf. Foulet, *Petite syntaxe* . . . , para. 446–488.

[3] The glossaries in many editions of O.F. texts are quite insufficient for your use, especially in the case of some volumes of the *Classiques*

eccentric forms : you will then know that *cose, rique, lie,* for example, are merely the Northern forms for Francien *chose, riche, liée*—and then you will not even need to look them up. If you still have to look for a dialectal form in the dictionary, enter the Francien form in your note-book as well. You will also save yourself much annoyance if, as you search the dictionary, you remember that medieval spelling was not as rigid as it is to-day. Be ready to find a word spelt in your text with a double consonant entered in the dictionary with a single consonant, and vice versa; a word with the suffix *-eïer* in an entry spelt *-oïer*, etc.

All this will require much work on your part; it will however, be very much worth your while, for it will at least, I hope, lead you to understand why, already in the 13th century, an Italian spoke of contemporary French as the ' parleure la plus delitable ', and a compatriot of ours, writing in Anglo-Norman, described it as ' la plus bel et la plus gracious language et plus noble parler apres latin d'escole, qui soit au monde '.[1]

Historical Philology

In most Universities students of French are expected to study the history of the language in its pronunciation (historical phonetics), in its forms—declensions, conjugations—(morphology), in the use of these forms (syntax), and in its vocabulary. And it is here, I think, that students most often fail to profit from their work, because they fail to view the material placed before

français du moyen age. You will therefore need to consult the specialized dictionaries. The most convenient of the smaller ones is R. Grandsaignes d'Hauterive, *Dictionnaire d'ancien français.* The standard, larger works to consult are F. Godefroy, *Dictionnaire de l'ancienne langue française . . . ,* 10 vols., with a supplement in volumes VIII–X; and Tobler-Lommatzsch, *Altfranzösisches Wörterbuch.*

[1] Two other books may be recommended. If you have difficulty in memorising O.F. forms, you can turn to D. Paton, *Manuel d'ancien français.* This very elementary book contains a summary of O.F. (unfortunately of rather an early date, the beginning of the 12th century) with exercises in the points dealt with. The attempt to write O.F. of your own will speedily drive the points home. If you read German and like the slow, empirical approach to language, you might prefer K. Voretzsch, *Einführung in das Studium der Altfranzösischen Sprache.* This is really a long linguistic explication of the *Pélerinage de Charlemagne à Jérusalem,* with all the linguistic forms dealt with as they arise in the text, the rules deduced and then systematized.

them in the right light and to work at it in a sensible fashion. So often the student feels that he is dealing with a series of formulas unrelated to the rest of his work, whereas a little reflexion should show that this side of his language work is a necessary prelude to his study of literature, and that, far from consisting of arid formulas to be memorized, language is a product of man in society and is as such affected by psychological, social and cultural factors.

The writer's only tools and his only medium are words : he relies on their sound, their forms, their various meanings, their use and ordered arrangement to convey all he wishes to say or suggest. Hence the frequency with which writers have spoken their minds on language problems : the Pléiade wished to enrich and 'illustrate' the French language and tried to show how this could be achieved; Montaigne, for all he says that he is no artist, deals with linguistic questions (e.g. the use of provincialisms); while in the 17th century the grammarians and classical writers were for ever concerned with grammar and between them creating modern French. That century is indeed critical from the linguistic point of view : fail to understand what was then attempted and done in that sphere and you will never fully appreciate the special qualities of French or of its classical writers. Instead you will regard French from a purely English point of view and so find it thin and anaemic, colourless and lacking in any richness. It is, too, only against the abstract, rational language of the 17th century that the new attitude to language evinced by the Romantics is properly to be understood and that the new ventures in poetic vocabulary can be fully appreciated.[1] But quite apart from its literary use, historical philology is of interest both in itself and as an expression of the mentality of the French people. The following remarks should help you to see its importance to you who, as an Arts student, are presumably interested in man and in everything connected with him.

In your study of *historical phonetics*, you should be on the alert to avoid considering sound changes as arbitrary, unmotivated

---

[1] Much valuable information can be gathered from the volumes so far published of F. Brunot, *Histoire de la langue française des origines à* 1900.

and unrelated; your task is, on the contrary, to seek to understand the processes of the particular phenomenon in question, the probable reasons for its occurrence and the connexion it has with other related sound changes. For example, it is of little value to learn ' tonic blocked *e* + nasal consonant >*ã* ' and leave it at that, as many students do. You need to consider it first as an example of assimilation or unconscious economizing of effort on the part of the speaker : the velum or soft palate is kept raised when you articulate a pure oral vowel and lowered for a nasal sound. In French when a vowel preceded a nasal consonant, speakers developed the habit of lowering the velum while still pronouncing the vowel, that is, they anticipated the lowering of the velum necessary for the nasal consonant. In this way there was a progressive nasal colouring of the oral vowel, and, instead of the sequence of oral and nasal articulation, there was at last merely continuous nasal pronunciation. All of which shows straight away that at least an outline knowledge of phonetics[1] is a necessary preliminary to the study of phonology. Further you must understand why an *e* became *ã* and not *ẽ*, that is, the vowel was not only nasalised but also lowered—and that should lead you to find out how low vowels tend to be nasalized more easily than high ones.

You must also, I have said, associate related phenomena. In this way what happens to tonic blocked *e* before a nasal is linked with what happens to other vowels similarly placed, even if in your text-book, say Bourciez, *Précis historique de phonétique française*, the vowels are considered separately. If you do this you will see that sound changes fall into patterns : nasalization, palatalization, dipthongization, and so on. Incidentally, everything becomes so much easier to learn this way, just because related facts are always more easily memorized than isolated ones. But your associations can be widened and your study made more interesting still. Many phonetic phenomena represent universal tendencies (assimilation, metathesis, etc.) and should be

[1] A good summary of the relevant parts of phonetics will be found in M. K. Pope, *From Latin to Modern French*, pp. 49-71. See also Brunot et Bruneau, *Précis de grammaire historique*, pp. 1–22. A more serious account of phonetics is to be found in M. Grammont, *Traité de phonétique*.

studied as such. For example, the Gauls and the French will seem a little less perverse in their phonetic habits if you link *vec'lum* for *vetulum* with the Cockney's *lickle* for *little*, or *ord* (*horridum*) with his '*Arry* : *vida* (*vita*) with the American's *Bridish*, or O.F. *jour* (*diurnum*) with *Injun* (*Indian*) or *ensemble* (*insimul*) with *brambles* (O.E. *bramles*).

You have, then, to see *how* sounds change : you will also try as far as it is possible to see why they change at all and why at a particular moment. For example, why should modern French have 16 different vowels while Spanish and Italian have only seven, when all three languages derive from Latin ? And when did this divergence take place ? At least part of the answer lies in the mixture of peoples that took place in France. The Celtic-speaking inhabitants (the substratum) are partly responsible; taking their phonetic habits into the new Latin tongue, they seem to have introduced the nasal vowels; while the German invaders with their particular speech habits (the sharp differentiation of tonic and atonic syllables, of short and long vowels) influenced the pronunciation of the native speakers (hence the splitting of tonic vowels in open position, etc.). The result was an Old French with a system of nearly thirty vowels, diphthongs and triphthongs. Such are the types of questions you should be continually asking as you study phonology, and such, very briefly, the type of answer you should seek.

Morphology is concerned with the forms of a language (its declension and conjugation systems mainly), while *syntax* deals with the use to which these forms are put. They are best studied together : in any case, they are only artificially separable. Here again the association of phenomena and the rational explanation of changes is the aim. You will learn, for example, that in later Old French (1) final consonants ceased to be pronounced (a phonetic or phonological fact); (2) the two-case declension system disappeared (a morphological fact); and (3) word order was tending to become fixed in its modern form, subject-verb-object, although this order did not become obligatory till later (a syntactical fact). These three phenomena should be linked together. When final *s* fell in pronunciation, with other final consonants, the O.F. declension system was, other things remaining unaltered, doomed, since it was precisely this -*s* that served to distinguish the cases. Further the relative freedom of word order in Old French depended to a large extent on the use of the declension system, since this served to indicate the mutual relationship of the substantives in the sentence. So, when it become impossible to distinguish subject and object by declension endings, free word order would lead to ambiguity (if subject and object could be put in any order, what would *le père punit le fils* mean ?), and was abandoned in favour of the fixed sequence subject-verb-object.

Here as elsewhere, you are concerned with a human product, that will shed some light on those who use it. Although linguistic change is often caused by factors which are beyond man's apparent control,[1] you will also find frequent evidence of man's inventiveness and of his mental processes as he deals with morphological and syntactical problems. Faced with the virtual loss of the Latin future tense (for phonetic reasons), speakers gave up using *legemus*, for example, when they wanted to say 'we shall read' and adopted *legere habemus*. This had at first a modal value ('we have to read') but soon became a purely future tense. You can trace the mental growth of the linguistic community as it advanced from parataxis, the simple juxtaposition of sentences, to hypotaxis, with interdependence of clauses made explicit by conjunctions (of concession, hypothesis, etc.).[2] But the most common mental habit in the realms of morphology (and elsewhere) is that of analogy. Children and the uneducated are, of course, always giving examples of this process : if we can say *I work*, *I worked*, then why not *I go*, *I goed ?* You will find that much morphological change in Old French is to be explained in terms of analogy : even gender can be affected by the form of the noun, as in e.g., *la sentinelle* and O.F. *la Pape*.

[1] For example, phonetic developments in popular Latin (change of vowel system, loss of final *m*, *s*) seriously affected the declension system, caused the future indicative of certain verbs to be identical in form with the present indicative, etc.

[2] Cf., for example, *Jo ai tel gent, plus bele ne vereiz*, Chanson de Roland, v. 564. Of course, parataxis is itself no proof of cultural insufficiency : English makes continual use of it !

There remains the history of French vocabulary. This can be studied from various points of view: what was the original form of the words? were they part of the 'hereditary stock' of the language or are they the result of borrowing? how has French been enriched by the formation of new words? and how have words changed in their meanings? It will be enough if we consider here only *etymology* (the study of the origins of words) and *semantics* (concerned with the changing meanings of words).

The usual practice in etymological study is to trace the French word back to its Latin (or Celtic or Germanic) source. Thus *pierre* is referred back to its Latin etymon *petra*, *caillou* to Celtic *caljo*; *champ* goes back to Latin *campus* and *sillon* to Celtic *selj*. But this is not enough; you need to discover why in each pair of words one is of Latin extraction and the other of Celtic origin: how is it that *sillon* was not taken from Latin and *champ* expressed by a Celtic word?[1] Even within the Latin field there are many such questions: why should *jour* go back to *diurnus*, and *dies* survive hardly at all in French and then only in combination (*midi*, *lundi*, etc.)? There is thus more to etymology than the mere search for the etymon: you must be ready to refer back to social and other conditions and to call in all your knowledge of semantics. Further, even if *chaque mot a son histoire*, words do not live in isolation, but in groups, and this fact has to be continually borne in mind when you are studying the history of a word. For example, by normal phonetic change Latin *exspectare* (look out for, wait for) became identical in form with *spectare* (look at). These two ideas still needed to be distinguished and speakers began to cast around in these words' neighbourhood for others that would serve their purpose: thus *spectare* was replaced by *mirari* (Spanish *mirar*) or by the Germanic *wardon* (French *regarder*): while *exspectare* was replaced by the new compound *ad-spectare* (Italian *aspettare*), by *sperare* in African Latin (Spanish *sperar*) or by *attendere* in Gaul (French *attendre*).

[1] The reason is, briefly, that the Gauls in rural areas, faced with Roman masters in the towns, tended to use the Latin word for, e.g., general geographical features, and to keep their own (Celtic) terms for objects of more purely agricultural application. Cf. Wartburg, *Problèmes et méthodes de la linguistique*, pp. 96–97. Wartburg deals with many of the problems raised in this section.

Semantics[1] reveals more clearly than any other aspect of linguistics the connexion between speech and speaker. A change of meaning may result from a change in the nature of the object, the concept of which the word evokes : or it may be caused by a change in the mental, moral or spiritual outlook of the speaker or by changing social conditions; and finally semantic change may depend on purely formal (phonetic) factors. Much of the material you gather will seem to consist of isolated facts, but it is your task to classify such facts, to systematize them—and the headings just given are as useful as most for such classification. As examples, consider the following. The concept *house* has been very variously named as the nature of the object has changed with changing social and political conditions : in the invasions the patrician's *domus* is destroyed and the word disappears : the peasant's *casa* remains, but later, as society becomes stable and more prosperous, it is replaced by *mansionem*, by *hospitalem* and so on. Changes in social organisation are seen in the variation in meaning in titles : consider the history of the group *senior, dominus, domina : seigneur, sire, monsieur, monseigneur, don, dame, madame.* Similarly, while Latin had two words to express the relationship ' uncle ', one for the father's brother, one for the mother's, and two words to express ' aunt ', French has only one word in each case : to *avunculus* and *patruus* corresponds *oncle*, to *matertera* and *amita, tante.* The explanation is that Roman law distinguished between the father's relatives and the mother's and needed separate words for them; in France no such legal differentiation was made and speakers abandoned unnecessary distinctions of form. To study completely the semantic changes brought about by variations in mental, moral and cultural attitude, would mean a complete study of the history of France : it is enough here if we think of Old French with many of its metaphors derived from the life and preoccupations of the nobility (hunting : *acharner, appât, hagard, nice* . . .), the growing abstraction of vocabulary due to the concern with the moral rather than the

[1] See Nyrop, *Grammaire historique* . . . , Vol. IV; the two books of S. Ullmann, *The Principles of Semantics* and *Précis de sémantique française* deal respectively with the general theory and its application to French.

43

picturesque in literature and so, perhaps, finally to the religious nature of French society; of the 16th century, when the widening of outlook led to a great increase in the vocabulary of French by widespread word-borrowing and creation, with consequent semantic confusion; of the 17th century with its attempts to eliminate this confusion in the interests of an over-riding desire for clarity : and so on. But man is not completely master : phonetic change may compel him to make vocabulary changes, and here you see man's inventiveness and resourcefulness at work. Take, for example, the now classical case of the Gascon cat and the cock.[1] In Gascony, for purely phonetic reasons, *gallus* (cock) and *cattus* (cat) fell together to give a common *gat*. Now it is obvious that, in a rural community at least, a single word for two objects in the same sphere of thought is likely to lead to confusion and trouble. The speakers of this region, therefore, while keeping *gat* for the cat, used either the humorous *bigey* (curate) or the arbitrary *aza* (pheasant) for the cock. The form of the word may affect the very attitude of the speaker towards the object whose concept is evoked by that word. Thus *perce-oreille* was originally so called because the insect's tail had the shape of the instrument used in ear-piercing; with the decline in the practice of piercing ears and the increasing rarity of that instrument, the word has been misinterpreted and led to the popular belief that the insect does actually enter the ear.

In this field of study then, you will find a wealth of fascinating material and your interest is assured. You should have no difficulty provided you can pass beyond the anecdotal to organise your material and see the continual connexion between the word and the man who utters it.

[1] This example comes from the work of J. Gilliéron, who, after producing the *Atlas linguistique de la France* in co-operation with E. Edmont, wrote a series of studies of what is called Linguistic Geography. This is not the place to describe his methods and his conclusions, but if you would like to see just how rich and complex language is and how closely bound up with man's life and work, then you should read some of his writings. See, for example, J. Gilliéron and M. Roques, *Etudes de géographie linguistique d'après l'Atlas linguistique de la France*; J. Gilliéron, *Généalogie des mots qui désignent l'abeille* . . . See also the very readable *Words and Sounds in English and French* by Prof. John Orr.

Linguistics

In addition to the courses on Old French and the History of the French language, you may be offered lectures on other aspects of French linguistics : on stylistics, on the structure of present-day French, on the work of linguistic geography, and so on. So many different courses are possible that we cannot hope to deal with them individually here. All that can be done is to offer some general remarks.

First, you would do well to read at least one book on the nature of linguistic study. Particularly valuable to you is likely to be R.-L. Wagner, *Introduction à la linguistique française.* In the introduction, *Linguistique et linguistique française* (pp. 15-57), the author, with French students in mind, treats of the problems and aims of modern language work; the rest of the book consists of a very useful critical bibliography. Also very illuminating is W. von Wartburg, *Problèmes et méthodes de la linguistique.*[1]

Secondly, you must realize what the term ' grammar ' means to the linguist. At school you may have studied grammar—if at all—as a means of learning ' correct usage '. You were told, perhaps, that English grammar demands that the same case should follow the verb ' to be ' as precedes it : so that ' It is me ' is wrong and only ' It is I ' is admissible. Similarly in French *se rappeler de quelque chose* will be proscribed in favour of *se rappeler quelque chose.* The point of view adopted by the grammarian in such cases may be empirical, as when he takes as his norm the language of a certain class of society,[2] or it may be *a priori* as when he forms a certain conception of the human mind and assumes that the structure of a language embodies—or should

[1] If you find this part of your work especially attractive, you can read one of these more general books : L. R. Palmer, *Introduction to Modern Linguistics*; J. Marouzeau, *La linguistique*; A. Dauzat, *La philosophie du langage.* The following have a wider range ; J. Vendryès, *Le langage, introduction linguistique à l'histoire* ; O. Jespersen, *Language*; L. Bloomfield, *Language*; A. Meillet, *Linguistique générale et linguistique historique.*

[2] Vaugelas in his *Remarques sur la langue françoise* (1647) took as his norm ' la façon de parler de la plus saine partie de la Cour, conformément à la façon d'escrire de la plus saine partie des Autheurs du temps.' Grévisse, *Le bon usage,* already recommended, is the best modern example of this approach.

embody—the universal principles of logic.[1] It is assumed, for example, that a sentence, like a logical proposition, must have a subject and a predicate. Such grammar is ' normative ', and to judge by the way the French press continues to devote columns to points of grammar and language, there is still great interest in such value judgements in France.

But the linguist of today will normally approach the grammar of a language in a different spirit. He will see himself as a scientist who must be as objective as, for example, a botanist faced with a new species of plant that does not fit his classification. As such, the linguist will not legislate or tell the users of the language what they are to do in given circumstances; nor will he impose on it an alien pattern (that of logic, for instance, or of another language such as Latin). He will rather accept the speech of a given community and seek to describe, correlate and explain its grammatical features. This he may do in a number of ways. He may start from the viewpoint of the speaker (or writer) who needs to express his thoughts : he will thus proceed from the thought to the external sign (sentence, word, sound) which expresses it.[2] He may, on the other hand, look at the speech-act from the opposite angle—that of the listener (or reader) who proceeds from the external sign to the underlying thought.[3] But there is yet another viewpoint and method. The grammarian may attempt to separate out the purely grammatical elements of the language, define them and show how they function within the language. G. Gougenheim had done this for French by the technique of ' functional opposition ' : that is to say, he opposes one grammatical feature to another (one tense of a verb to another, one mood to another, prepositions such as *par/pour*, *dès/depuis*, etc.) and by the contrast is able to define the function of each.[4]

[1] Since logic is universal and such grammar is based on logic, some writers have striven to create a universal, logical grammar. Lancelot attempted this in his *Grammaire générale et raisonnée* or *Grammaire du Port-Royal* of 1660.

[2] Such is the attitude of F. Brunot in *La pensée et la langue.*

[3] J. Damourette and Ed. Pichon have so studied French in their long work, *Des mots à la pensée, essai de grammaire de la langue française.* They study French as the expression of the subconscious of the individual French speaker.

[4] G. Gougenheim, *Système grammatical de la langue française.* It

46

Thirdly, you must avoid the common error of considering linguistics as a body of agreed material studied by all linguists in the same way. The books just mentioned will safeguard you against such a misconception, but more must be said. There are indeed a number of ways in which students of language have viewed and still view the subject-matter of their science.[1] We have already seen two of these : the historical method which triumphed in the 19th century by tracing the sound- (and other) changes by which European languages developed from a common Indo-European origin (an approach best illustrated by the ' Neo-Grammarians ', e.g. Meyer-Lübke, A. Tobler); and linguistic geography, which records varieties of dialect from region to region, from commune to commune (Gilliéron). Against the historical method there have been two main reactions. One school, the Idealists, led by Karl Vossler, corrected the very 19th-century tendency of the Neo-Grammarians to treat language as a physical product, obeying natural laws like those of physics, by viewing it as an expression of the spirit of man, both as a member of a cultural community and as an individual. They see language, then, as both a cultural fact (in the community) and as an aesthetic fact (in the individual speaker and writer).[2] The second of these attitudes leads naturally to one form of Stylistics, a separate branch of language study.[3]

was the Prague School of Phonologists who first developed this technique of opposition; they used it to study the functional values of phonemes or speech sounds. For French see G. Gougenheim, *Eléments de phonologie française*.

[1] For an excellent account of these different viewpoints see I. Iordan, *An Introduction to Romance Linguistics, its Schools and Scholars*, trans. J. Orr.

[2] The cultural or ' external ' history of French is best studied in works by non-Idealists : F. Brunot, *Histoire de la langue française*, and W. v. Wartburg, *Evolution et structure de la langue française*. Vossler's own book *Langue et culture de la France*, trans. A. Juilland is interesting, but must be read very critically.

[3] Many now make a distinction between the study of an author's style, and Stylistics which ' étudie les faits d'expression du langage au point de vue de leur contenu affectif ' (Bally, *Traité de stylistique française*, t. I, p. 16). The first studies the speech of an individual, the second the language of the community. Good introductions to Stylistics are : J. Marouzeau, *Précis de stylistique française*, P. Guiraud, *La stylistique*, and M. Cressot, *Le style et ses techniques*.

47

Another group, the followers of Ferdinand de Saussure in Geneva, has rehabilitated the ' descriptive ' approach which the successes of historical linguistics tended to discredit. In this view there are two methods equally open to the linguist—he may study development in time (historical or diachronistic linguistics), or he may investigate a language at a certain stage in its history without reference to what went before or came after (descriptive or synchronistic linguistics) : each method is legitimate, but distinct. Saussure, in his desire to arrive at a knowledge of the structure of a language, at an essence rather than at the accidents, gave precedence to descriptive study. Users of a language are very seldom conscious of the past history of the sounds and forms they employ; for them sounds and forms go together to form a stable unity, and it is thus, Saussure held, that a language should be studied.[1] But the divorce of synchronism and diachronism has not been made absolute, and some linguists have been working to bring the two parties together again. Wartburg,[2] for example, has shown the need to weld the two methods.

There is not then one fixed, immutable method of linguistic study. Indeed you, in your work, will need to use both the historical and descriptive methods : what is important is to keep both methods separate and to realize just what you are doing, which approach you are adopting at any one moment. Indeed, consciousness of what he is doing, and why, is the distinguishing feature of the good student always.

And finally, the general advice given about other language work applies here too : your task is to study language rationally and not mechanically—to see how linguistic phenomena are

[1] Cf. F. de Saussure, *Cours de linguistique générale*. This book was published by two of Saussure's pupils, A. Séchehaye and Ch. Bally, from notes they had taken of his lectures. The body of structural studies has grown in recent years. Perhaps the most useful is Ch. Bally, *Linguistique générale et linguistique française*. This type of study is dealt with in two books already referred to : Wagner's *Introduction* and Wartburg's *Problèmes et méthodes*. . . . The best way to compare the historical and descriptive approach is to read together two such works as : K. Sneyders de Vogel, *Syntaxe historique du français* and L. Foulet, *Petite syntaxe de l'ancien français*.
[2] Cf. his *Problèmes et méthodes*, . . . pp. 7–11 and particularly 123–177.

related and not separate and isolated facts, to remember that language is a human product and therefore influenced in its development by the psychology of the speaker, by his society, by his history.

2. THE STUDY OF LITERATURE

I have said that nobody can learn for you; certainly no-one can read for you, and the study of literature is obviously, before all else, reading books. But books—even of our own day—need trained faculties to understand them in the fulness of their meaning and to appreciate them in the fulness of their excellence; and they need explanations when they were written in another age, in another form of the language, in the middle of different ideas, hopes, anxieties and beliefs. All of this you could get, by long and careful work, from good editions and the best of up-to-date criticism and history.

But you cannot learn to know the whole of French literature by yourself in one, two or three years. Your syllabus sets you limits (probably), and it provides instruction —in detail, on certain prescribed texts (to direct and facilitate the work you still must do yourself), and in a more general form, on the history of certain periods of literature.

If you take these courses as guides and not as substitutes for your work you need little help from outside; but a few warnings can be given which may save you from mistaken attitudes of mind, liable to spoil your work and falsify your ideas.

Set books

This is the part of your literary work of which the aims are clearest—to know what is in the books, and to be able to discuss it adequately—but it is not the easiest. It is perhaps the most valuable, not only because of the books you come to know, but also because here is your training in the art of reading—the greatest challenge to those powers of sharp observation and clear judgement which you have to develop.

The principal help you can derive from teaching here (apart from the explanation of difficulties) is knowing what,

D

in a given work, will repay your close study. It may not be the ideas (in a poem), it may not be the story (in a novel). Whatever the critical judgements suggested by lecturers or other books, your business is not to learn them and repeat them parrot-fashion, but to look out for the features they mention when you read the text, to see if you can make their appreciations your own (and if not, not to be afraid to say so). Otherwise they will close your mind, and spoil your reading; but used as I have said, they enrich the experience of reading and sharpen your perceptions for the future.

But when you read your texts, keep your attention on them. First make sure of the meaning—not only of each sentence, but of the whole, as point leads to point. Then, do your best to enter into the spirit of the author, let him carry you away by the eloquence of his pleading, by the beauty of his vision or simply of his language, or by the profundity of his interpretation of some action, some situation real or imagined. (Remember, you may not agree with his views; but you will lose a lot if you do not put aside your own while you honestly try to grasp his. Bring up your own objections at a later stage, when you are trying to form a general impression and a final judgement; try to see what his answer would be; and remember it is wise to be very humble in contradicting one who has experienced more, and very likely reflected more, than you have.)

Then, in a later reading, and more coldly, go back and try to see *how* he affected you as he did.

This approach will determine the kind of notes you make on your set books. It is very desirable to analyse the argument step by step—if there is a sustained argument which gives the book its importance; but it is often useless to summarize a novel episode by episode—unless your attention has been directed to its construction. Often notes on meaning, and page-references to passages which struck you as useful for quoting as examples of the author's characteristics, will suffice.

One important detail: you cannot appreciate French

poetry if you cannot scan it. The principles are given, rather lengthily but well, in H. E. Berthon, *Nine French Poets*; and baldly and rather badly in some other introductions to texts you may have used. The standard work is M. Grammont, *Petit traité de versification française*. You may think you know them, but few students really do. Unless you master the sometimes intricate technicalities (based on bygone pronunciations) governing the count of syllables, you will infuriate examiners by quoting metrical monstrosities, and had better not quote at all.

But another part of the theory is not mere technicality— if you cannot catch the rhythm you might as well be reading prose. The so-called monotonous ' classical ' alexandrine has a more variable rhythm than any English metre; for stress, which makes the rhythmical pattern, occurs in French on the last sounded syllable of any breath-group, long or short. (Other kinds of stress do not count in versification). Each pause creates a stress. Pauses usually come after the 6th and 12th syllables, but these may not be the only ones, nor the most marked. A typical line will have 4 ' beats ', but it is rare to find them in the same places in successive lines, and there may be more or fewer (whereas in English the number is theoretically fixed). In principle each breath-group has the same duration, like bars in music; so a long group is spoken rapidly, a short group is slow, or compensated by the pause.

The only way to make sure of your prosody is to make sure of the syllable-count and rhythmic divisions of every line you read, as you read it. Some French readers of verse mark the rhythm carefully, and are useful to listen to; others make the verse-pattern difficult to follow for beginners—but when you can follow this freer style of declamation, you will have got the feel of French poetry.

Explication

My remarks on reading texts must have seemed vague without examples, but to provide examples is the function of the exercise called *explication de textes* (or *explication litté-*

raire), which it is to be hoped you will not only hear done in lectures, but be called upon to do yourself. It is valuable as a test; but even more as a training in observation and method. It can best de defined as a lesson or a test in the art of reading.

In point of fact the aims, rules and plans suggested by different writers on *explication* are not quite uniform. It is a regular part of secondary as well as advanced education in France, and for this reason the advice of French writers is addressed to students far more schooled in the art than British students can become—until it is taught, as I should like to see it, not only in our sixth forms for French, but from fourth forms upwards, and for English as well.[1]

Let us begin with the general purpose—to show that you have understood and appreciated a literary passage, i.e. to set down :

　　what the author is saying;

　　what this means and implies, and why it is interesting;

　　what, over and above that, he makes you feel (or wants to);

　　and *how* he sets about this (which is the most delicate point).

The plan you use is optional (unless a fixed framework is laid down in your department). I recommend four divisions which, sometimes under other names, are much the same as you will find described elsewhere—Context, Analysis,

[1] The advice given in Bouvier et Jourda, *Guide de l'étudiant* . . ., is complicated with considerations the British student is not often asked to deal with.

G. Rudler, *L'explication française*, makes the method so microscopic as to be in some ways discouraging. Much more elementary, P. E. Phillips and J. B. Davies, *French Appreciation for Sixth Forms*, give a useful summary of points to look for, in the form of questions.

B. Schlumberger, *L'explication littéraire*, is equally good on the university level, though her examples gush too much and criticize too little.

R. A. Sayce, *Style in French Prose*, will open many eyes to the amount to be learnt from the study of words and constructions.

The advice given here is simpler than all these, but it is adequate, I believe, for the exercise as practised anywhere in this country, and for the usual type of examination question calling for ' analysis ' of a passage, ' context and allusions ', and a ' commentary on form and subject-matter '.

Matter, Manner. Alternatives are, to combine the last three and take the passage section by section, once you have ' placed ' it in its context, from beginning to end (often the most convenient method in a lecture), or, better, to combine the last two only, after analysing the whole. (It is often hard to disentangle Matter and Manner—they are not two distinct realities, but two aspects of the same thing, a piece of writing. However, they stand for two different sets of questions, both of which must be tackled.) But the four divisions make it easier to bring out a few important points clearly. The *explication* should ideally have as much unity as the *dissertation*, proceeding from section 1, stating where the passage occurs, and section 2, summarizing what it says, to 3, the discussion of what it says, and 4, the demonstration that the way of saying it is appropriate and reinforces what has to be conveyed.

Context. In an examination on a set book, this includes name of author, title and date of work, approximate place in the work; then, all that must be known to understand the passage (either about characters, events or ideas in the work —' new readers start here '—or about details of contemporary life or previous history referred to). In class-work much of this can obviously be abridged : avoid in any case the temptation to summarize the whole book. The only difficulty about this section is to keep it short. But from this point the whole passage should need no further reference to anything outside it; and from now on it is a fault to trespass outside it—except, of course, for comparisons.

Analysis. An analysis is not a rambling, inexact and sometimes incomplete paraphrase, in shambling English, of a piece of careful and elegant French. (Paraphrase, even good, has no place *anywhere* in an *explication*.) To analyse is to lay bare the author's plan—its main lines, and its subsidiary details—in his order; this, and nothing more. But this includes showing the ' thread ' of thought that runs through the passage, on which (if it is well composed) everything hangs in its place. It is easy to pick one conspicuous idea from each section, and exhibit these in such words that no connexion is visible between them—no reason why this or that item should be there at all, or why it should not have come before, instead of after, some other. If this criticism can be made of your analysis, you have probably failed to see the ' thread ' yourself.

It is almost certain that you will find the author had a conscious plan. If you really cannot find one, then show, still by analysing step by step, that the author is repeating himself, or digressing and returning (Montaigne will do this). If true, it is likely to be important.

A narrative plan is easy to see and dissect (how each step is prepared for, and necessary for the next); the plan of a lyrical poem hardly more difficult (movement from theme to theme, and if possible how the movement—the transition —is managed); in a philosophical passage the author will obviously be working from the problem he has set himself to its solution, or from a set of premisses to a conclusion, by logical steps you ought to be able to recognize. Scenes and even speeches in plays are planned—the playwright is work-ing towards some incident or some effect, and has not unlimited time to let his characters ramble. In the 17th century especially, digression is a fault, and the speeches are as carefully laid out as the plots; even when it would be natural for a character to be incoherent or repetitive in some emotional crisis, you find—under a surface show of confusion—that he adopts the same order an orator would have adopted in cold blood for the most effective presentation of whatever was to be said.

Show that you see both the unity of the whole and the order of the parts by (1) summing up the whole drift of the passage in one statement and then (2) dividing it (using line-references or quoting first and last words of sentences) into the sections you have found, with a sentence of summary for each. Up to the nineteenth century ' Rhetoric' was taught in all schools; and the headings prescribed by Rhetoric were : exordium (introduction), proposition (the point to be made), division (plan), narration (statement of the facts at issue), confirmation (proofs, arguments), refutation (of the adversary's case, really made or imagined), recapitulation, and peroration (conclusion). Not all will necessarily be present, of course, and the order may vary. (You are not in the least obliged to use these terms). Keep this section as concise as possible—all comment comes later.

Matter. While you should aim here to extract all the meaning in your passage (and nothing that is not in it, however prominent in the rest of the book), you must decide what are the one or two important points (reducible if possible to the different aspects of one point) to which you ought to call attention; anything unconnected with these should be dismissed in a very few words. What these points are, is for you to find. Whatever you know in advance about the author and book may help you. The answer varies, obviously, with the nature of the passage. In extreme cases (some lyrical verse or poetic prose) it may suffice to point out how slender the matter is, before passing on (in section 4) to what will then be the much more vital subject, the art with which it is treated.

If you are at a loss what to say, read the passage again, closely and slowly, pondering every phrase and every word. Students rarely get close enough to their text.

What you should probably examine and discuss, in a philosophical or discursive passage, is : the statements the author makes, the assumptions behind these, the logic (or lack of logic) of the arguments used, the sources of the ideas if you know them, and any alterations made by the borrower, the implications of these ideas (what follows if they are true ? —Implications drawn by the writer, or by critics or by you ? Make it clear which). You may if you wish attempt to refute or qualify them. Finally you may be able to connect them with others in books by the same writer, his contemporaries, or his disciples. (For such purposes you may look outside the boundary of the passage, and it is good to do so; provided you started from something inside it.)

In fiction (novel or drama), look at the personages—what they are made to reveal in the passage (not elsewhere, unless for comparison) about themselves, or others (or the author, if you think his ideas or his temperament are showing through); discuss character and motives, the ideals of conduct which are appealed to or infringed (remembering that the author's judgement of his creations, and his philosophy of life, may not be yours, and are much more important than yours because he is he and you are only you—though yours have a right to be heard, afterwards, with modesty). Look at the events, as he imagines or reproduces them—what he emphasizes or passes over; how he makes one lead to another; what tragic, comic or other impression he is building up. (This is a different matter from the 'effects' of style, though you should find these working towards the same end). If there is a source, historical or otherwise, or a reference to the author's own experience, direct or disguised, consider how he selects, adapts, suppresses or invents details—and why—and attempt a judgement. (But in all cases of 'sources' bear in mind (1) that it is extremely rare, perhaps impossible, for a plot or an idea to be created out of nothing, so that borrowing is only plagiarism when the borrower has done no work himself on his loan; and (2) that 'truth to history' is not always a high or necessary virtue—though something depends on the claims the author may have made.)

The questions to be asked and answered in this section are —'What is being said?' and 'Why?' and 'What then?'; in the next section, 'How?'

Manner. This is where students with a British lack of training fall down. The commonest approaches—all bad —are these three:

1. 'There is a metaphor in line 3, an antithesis in line 5, alliteration in line 7, enjambement between lines 9 and 10. . . .' A jumbled casual list of no interest to anyone. It would have been as useful to count the number of commas.

2. 'Chateaubriand is celebrated as the master of the melodious, rhythmical sentence. Here we see the sentences

are melodious and rhythmical.' The student writing this had found a critic to do his work for him, and he is so sure he has got hold of the right thing to say, that he makes it look as if he had not bothered to see whether the passage bore it out. If he had, he should have started from there, and cut out his first sentence. After he has shown, and tried to analyse, examples of melody and rhythm, then he may mention that they are characteristic of Chateaubriand.

3. ' The author almost makes us see the beauty of the scene.' ' We seem to feel . . . ' The intentions are all right here, but the result is empty gush. It is not enough to ' seem to feel ' ; you are expected to know what you feel and have a shot at describing it. (For those with too little taste, or perceptions too jaded, to feel anything, the only course is to try to guess from the evidence what he hoped they might feel.)

What you are made to feel is the subject of this section—and what makes you feel it. It is an ' effect ', of which the cause can only be the words in the passage (plus, perhaps, what precedes). You have been dealing with the information or ideas these words convey; but no writer is content to convey only that : he wants to make his reader respond—at the lowest, to be interested and convinced, at the highest, to share some experience with him or some character of his. Any passage in any book could be rewritten with ease so as to keep all the intellectual content and destroy all the emotive effect.

That is what style is—language used to produce some ' effect '. Images (vivid concrete words, whether figurative or not) appeal to the senses or imagination as well as the intelligence. Figures of speech using contrast or climax add vigour. Repetition and omission are means of directing attention where it is wished. Irony contrasts the real meaning with an apparent meaning which is different, and gives you the pleasure of ' seeing through it '. Devices of rhythm (including metre) and sound act on you through your inward ear—lull you or jerk you awake, and sometimes (not often)

57

suggest by imitation. In good writing these things are not mere ornament.

Certain 'effects' were not intended—some 'period' styles seem to us quaint or conventional just because expressions strike us differently after the changes that have occurred since (these are points to discuss when they arise) : but otherwise we must assume they were designed—though often perhaps the author chose his expressions by instinct and could not have given the technical explanation which you are expected to find.

So this is where the metaphor in line 3 and the antithesis in line 5 come in and make sense—when you think you can see, and say, why they are there.

There are two ways to start work : either ' This passage fills me with a feeling of . . .—How ? ' or ' There are rather a lot of (say) questions or exclamations here—Why?' Better use both, for any stylistic device that seems pointless may point to an intention you have not seen. Search attentively, read very closely (once again); remember all you know about the author's tendencies, and any clues you have about what critics have seen in the passage; listen to sound and rhythm.

Consider the choice of words (for authors can and do choose, and often change their minds). Where they are not merely natural and exact, are they abstract and philosophical—concrete and vivid—metaphorical (implying a comparison)—vague but emotionally charged—technical ? In descriptions, do they make you see or hear (colours, shapes, noises), or experience emotion (*solitaire*, *triste*), or understand or judge intellectually (*inégal*, *ridicule*) ? Which do most of the work, nouns, nouns plus adjectives, or verbs (stressing objects or qualities, or attitudes, movements, changes) ? Does one word, or a set of words of similar import, dominate the passage ?

Does the style change within the passage ? Do not rest till you understand why. (See an example in Appendix B (1) which throws light on the ' matter ' as well).

Can you, after all, find little to say about the ' style ' ? You may be right—not because the author was incompetent (one can comment on bad style), but because he was only concerned to write clearly for readers who might be supposed to be interested already (the importance lying in the ' matter '). If you think this is the case, say so. But he is probably betraying, in spite of himself, something of his character and turn of mind. His simplicity may be deliberate simplification (rejection of inessentials), which can be studied.[1] And he has presented his matter in some order —and no order is inevitable. His order may have allowed effects of contrast or climax which are not conspicuous and may seem inherent in what he is saying—yet another order would have thrown them away. This too is ' style '.

Now, after noting all your points, arrange them, either starting with the effect or effects produced and showing the means, or starting with the devices and leading up to a statement of the effect.

Observe four rules strictly :

1. Point out no device unless you can show how it contributes to an ' effect ';

2. Make no statement without illustrative quotation (or reference, by line-number or otherwise) to prove you saw what you describe;

3. Shun vagueness; ban such words as ' effective '—you have to say *what* effect you observe;

4. Shun hyperbole, here, and in all you write about literature. You are not expected to rave about authors—it always rings false. You will usually show good judgement if you admire them, for they have been carefully chosen, but you are not compelled to. The important thing is to show sense and taste in picking out the aspects to admire or criticize. (Of course there will be weak points, but you show poor taste if they blind you to the rest.) And avoid superlatives. There is no sense in writing that your book is the most beautiful, moving or profound of its kind that was ever composed—not even if you add ' probably ' : everyone knows you have not read all the others it could be compared with.

Finally there are the simple difficulties of interpretation : every obscure expression, every archaic form of speech, must be

[1] See Appendix B (ii).

investigated and explained. (Annotated editions and their glossaries give most of the help needed; the 'Editions des Grands Ecrivains' in your library have special 'lexiques'; there are special dictionaries for French of various periods, and standard books on historical grammar which your linguistic studies should have made you familiar with.) In class work, bring up yourself any difficulties you cannot explain. The tutor scores a point every time he is the first to point to a sentence you did not understand; two points, if you had not realized you did not understand it (and this happens constantly).

This explanatory part of your *explication* is best grouped in one paragraph, after the 'allusions', or at the beginning or end of the 'manner' section. Some teachers make the *explication linguistique* one of the most important parts of the whole thing; but then it becomes language work, not literary.

Conclusion. If you can do it without repetition or platitude, and if you have managed to find, in some degree, the unity I recommended, bring together here what you have been obliged to separate under 'analysis', 'matter' and 'manner', and sum up what one may learn about the author's merits, or intentions, or character.

After all these details, let me make one more attempt to define the purpose and method of *explication*. So many students who come fresh to it tell me midway through a year's work that they 'didn't understand quite what I wanted'. Put it this way: you have a set book, say a comedy of Molière, which you have to read, and want to understand and appreciate. A traditional course of teaching would provide you with ideas about the 'meaning' of the play, the characters in it, the sources of the comic effects, the sources (in the literary sense) of some of the episodes, the dramatic structure, the versification. The danger of all this, in the eyes of those who prefer to base study on *explication*, is that it tends to give ready-made answers which almost make it unnecessary to read the play at all; whereas a characteristic extract from the play, set for *explication*, can hardly fail to bring up several of these topics, and they will be the things you are expected to discuss. Only, this time, whatever you say about meaning, character, comedy or style must start from analysis of the specimen in front of you. You have to show that you have not merely been told about it, but seen and recognized it for yourself.

Explication is not easy, and I have not tried to make it seem so. Your first attempt may not succeed; but each *explication* you do, or hear given, should open your eyes to the wealth of meaning and feeling concealed in paragraphs you might not have thought worth reading twice—a wealth of which perhaps the author did not expect his reader to be fully conscious, of which he may not have been fully conscious himself : but your task here is to take his finished product to pieces and lay bare the works, if you can. Believe me, it will not spoil your enjoyment of it—rarely, even, for the short time you are working on it; and in return it will enrich your capacity for such enjoyment in the future.[1]

History of Literature

Scholars are not content to let the study of literature end with the careful reading of books. Particularly during the last hundred years, innumerable approaches have been tried out, based on philosophy (e.g. the nature of poetry and its use of language; the standards of judgement to apply) or on scientific conceptions (the search for causes and laws), or, most often perhaps, on history. Literature may be turned into documents for historians (but this is outside our subject); history may be used to illuminate literature, by relating authors, individually or collectively, to the life of their time—prevalent ideas and tastes, recent events, the writer's place in society, or the material circumstances and personal contacts of his private life. Biography has taken to private detectives' methods (the name of Molière's father's tenant, or of yet another woman courted by Balzac) with results that affect the interpretation of literature only indirectly, but sometimes interestingly (as with Flaubert's youthful love-episode). Life and works are made to contribute to a posthumous psycho-analysis of the author's personality. Finally, the history of literature itself has been attempted many times—the development of genres, themes, artistic theories, traditions, and the influence of writer on writer or book on book.

[1] Two specimen *explications* are given in Appendix B.

Some of these methods are still experimental, some have been given up, many are contested.[1] You will meet them in the scholarly studies you read, but as methods most of them are not for the undergraduate student. What you will, however, have to deal with to some extent is : (1) biographies of authors, (2) other background knowledge necessary to understand their works, and (3) some idea of the place of each in a development—the influences they experienced and the influence they exerted in their turn.

I shall confine myself to some warnings about the historical, non-literary element common to these three. It must be used, for books do not drop from heaven perfect and complete; artists and thinkers are usually more sensitive to environment than other men. Remember only that, while researchers may lay their emphasis where they please, you are a student of literature, not of history.

First, let me introduce a distinction which is vital, between historical fact and what is not fact but something else.

The only unquestionable facts that history presents are public records or other documents, with no motive for falsehood, attesting the date or the nature of some contemporary event fully known to the writer. References to such documents you can rely on because they can be checked—not that you will yourself look up the parish register recording (say) Racine's christening; but you can reasonably assume that you could if you had to.

Next in order come all other statements (e.g. in books or letters) by individuals about facts within their knowledge. These testimonies may carry great weight but they may be mistaken or untruthful—it has not been unknown for a writer to falsify the dates of his own poems (Hugo), to lie about his debt to another writer (Racine), or to embellish the details of his own actions (Chateaubriand).

Last come the statements of scholars and critics about events or people, which, except as far as they reproduce the two kinds of data described above, are merely the deductions of fallible humans making the most of the facts they have, and subject to prejudice

[1] A thorough, erudite and searching discussion can be found in R. Wellek and A. Warren, *Theory of Literature*.

and plain carelessness. Historical or critical judgements can never be certain, but at most probable. Some, generally accepted till recently, have now been upset; others will be to-morrow; some will always be hotly debated. On the great writers like Molière, Racine, Flaubert, and even more on ' difficult ' poets like Rimbaud, all the critics are at loggerheads with each other. Only the lazy student who makes do with one manual can remain long in ignorance of this fact. If you could check for yourself every demonstration of every critic you use—the accuracy and completeness of his data, and the logic of his deductions—you would be in a position to decide which one you supported. You cannot be asked to do all this; but you can notice the date of each work of criticism (then you may see, when you know some of the history of recent thought, what influences were at work in it); and I shall try to show in a moment how you can use the critics as aids without relying on them as authorities.

In a word, distinguish always between (1) what you know to be true, (2) what you know some witness has stated, and (3) what you know somebody else thinks; and trust only the first of these.

Now to consider the different uses of history in the study of literature.

First comes biography, the life, circumstances and career of individual authors. Historical *fact* can do little here but establish dates (birth, death, publications) and names (parents, wife, children, friends, etc.); it can disprove certain suppositions that could be made about relationships or intentions, but never prove them conclusively. (Thus, Rotrou's tragedy *Iphigénie* of 1640 *could not* have copied Racine's *Iphigénie* of 1674 : whereas Racine could have copied Rotrou—but did he ? He never confessed it. We can be pretty sure he did by comparing the texts; but this is a different kind of proof, and is never absolutely conclusive, since the resemblance *might* be coincidence). You probably know how the Romantic poets paraded their private sentiments in their verses—how difficult it is to write about Lamartine's *Méditations* without mentioning 'Elvire': you may not know that the facts are not quite as the poems state them, and the real importance of Julie Charles in Lamartine's life is—partly owing to Lamartine—not entirely certain. In other words we have here mainly, not facts, but statements by an interested party. In general, though we know how Lamartine, Musset or Vigny lived, we cannot say why they wrote the poems they wrote. Other contemporaries were disappointed in love and did not write similar works. Poets use imagination (and literary tradition) as well as genuine emotion and they never tell us the exact proportion. (Nor does the first person singular in a poem or story necessarily stand for the author in real life.) In any case the important thing is, how good a poem they write. Sincerity is not a literary criterion; biography may help to understand, but never to judge. An imitative poem may still be sincere; but a sincere poem may be bad, and a poem based on imagined emotions may be good. So Julie Charles is largely irrelevant to your study of *Le Lac*—but not quite, if comparison of the real Julie (so far as we know her) with the poetic Elvire helps us to guess the proportion of the different elements in Lamartine's lyrical work.

Now let us take the use of history of literature in ‘ survey courses ’, what I have called ‘ the panorama of French writing, with all that helps to explain it ’. You are likely to have surveys of stated periods, with the more important writers, in one or a few genres, fitted into their places in the history of a development.

It is important for you to realize early, before you take this kind of course for gospel, that *facts* are rare in the history of literary developments; some of it reposes on contemporary testimony (which we have seen to be not always reliable), and much of the rest on the interpretation and inference of modern critics—interpretations which have had to be revised several times already since literary history began to be written, and will be again. What you will listen to in lectures and read in commentaries is a perpetual to-and-fro from proved fact through doubtful testimony to personal opinion and back again.

Suppose you are told (to invent a synthetic example which will bring up most of the points I want to make): ‘ During this period the state of affairs in the country was so-and-so, men's minds were working on such and such problems; there arose a school of writers who believed this and that; the author X in

64

particular wished to show . . .; *and so* in this book of his you find . . .'

This kind of statement touches on political, economic or social history (which itself is not crude fact but a series of generalizations made by historians from the facts—each generalization liable to be qualified by other historians), on the history of thought (again summarized and generalized), and on the beliefs and aims of writers (based, sometimes on their statements, sometimes on modern critical opinions). It also contains the implication that the facts of history *caused* the beliefs and aims and therefore the writings—which as we have seen, opens up enormous questions, since we can never say for certain what makes a man write a book (or whether ' makes ' is the right word).

At every step, for the sake of clarity and simplicity, the imaginary lecturer's language has to pretend to be precise about realities that in the nature of things were confused and complex. ' This period ' is an arbitrary division of time, and was not uniform from start to finish. The summaries of the ' state of affairs ' and the ' ideas of the time ' depend on somebody's opinion of what elements were most important. The ' school ' of writers were people more or less in agreement on some, but not all, of their ideas, all for different lengths of time—or they may never have realized they were a school at all, and the expression may simply be a convenience for historians.[1]

So that by the time our lecturer has reached a particular book and purports to explain it by its background, he is giving a conjectural interpretation, which may be very probable, but may at any time be challenged by a new one.

A special danger for students is that this ' history ' is terribly liable to get more inaccurate as it is transmitted : uncertain to start with, it next has to be compressed and simplified for lecturing purposes—exceptions and fine distinctions are left out; and if a misunderstanding or a shift of emphasis creeps in as you take it down, memorize it, or reproduce it in an answer, the result may be complete falsehood.

---

[1] The *grands classiques* of the 17th century were first called so at the end of the 18th. Balzac was dead before he was called a realist. Flaubert refused to be called a realist or a naturalist, and Verlaine to be called a symbolist.

Nevertheless the method cannot be condemned, if only because there is no other way of arriving at any wide view of literature at all. It is legitimate for the scholar, who has (we hope) tested his facts and pondered his deductions. It is legitimate for the lecturer, who has (we hope) gone over the ground, if he is repeating somebody else, and checked at least some of the steps by what he knows from other sources. It is legitimate for you to use the same method in your turn—to use the method, but not to build on the results of someone else who has used it. ' What the sergeant said is not evidence,' according to lawyers : what Lanson (or another critic, or your lecturer) said is not a fact but an opinion, not ' what you know ' but ' what you know someone else thinks '.

You may, in an essay or examination answer, be asked (in effect) to repeat somebody else's demonstration—e.g. to show how X came to write his book. To do this you must follow the same steps once again—first, enough data to build on, then deductions, making the reasoning clear. But suppose the question is, to show what X wanted to express about a certain problem in his book. It looks like the same question, but it is a different and more interesting one—because it can, and should, be answered by starting from another and altogether more certain set of data than the ' state of affairs ' in X's time. This is probably the type of question you will meet more often than the ' historical ' one (I hope so at least).

Suppose, for example, the question is Corneille's conception of the hero or Molière's conception of comedy. Unwary students always start in the wrong way—' Corneille (or Molière) was a classicist '—they may or may not add: ' which means he held such and such beliefs about his art '—' and set out to show . . .' I stop them there, and ask ' How do you know what he set out to show ? ' All they know is that somebody else thinks, or thought, it was this—they are building on sand ; yet they were prepared to go on calmly ' *therefore* in *Horace* (or *Le Misanthrope*) he depicts . . . .' Unless their premisses are *facts*, that ' therefore ' is quite un-justified.

But, if you must not start from hearsay, what sort of facts

are within your knowledge, on which you can build without being met by this objection ? What, but the works of Corneille (or Molière, or X or Y) *which you have read* ? They are first-hand documents : you have eyes to read as well as Lanson or whoever it was. After all, that is where they started, to build their own theories of what the author ' set out to show '.

For my invented fragment of a lecture concealed (as many books and lectures do conceal) an important part of the process it was based on. After, or before, looking at the historical circumstances, the historian or critic looks at the author's books, and works out from them, independently (in theory) of all ' background ', what the author thought and felt on certain topics. If this ties up with what the background suggested that he might well have felt, each line of enquiry confirms the other and the investigator is content. (If sometimes he makes the evidence work out as he wants, that is just human imperfection.)

The historical line of enquiry is outside your scope, but the analysis of the book or books is right down your street, and that is where you must start. The student essays I quoted began the wrong way round, and used ' therefore ' when they should have used ' because '. The logical order is : ' We are looking for evidence on what Corneille thought about so-and-so. In *Horace* we find . . ., in *Cinna* we find . . ., in *Polyeucte* . . .; there is common ground here; *therefore* it seems reasonable to suppose that Corneille held . . .' First, the cases and examples throwing light on the question at issue; then, analysis and discussion; last, the ' inference ' (it is a logicians' technical term), the explanation which seems best to cover them.

This way, you have shown and used your own real knowledge· The conclusion you arrive at need not be new and original—that is a bit much to ask; it is yours nevertheless, because you have checked the steps, and, if you have been wise enough to read more than one critic, you have *chosen* the answer you adopt. The critics will help you to find and interpret your examples; you may even quote their opinions, but *in your conclusion*, when you have laid out the evidence which seems to you to show them to be true.

But are you at liberty to contradict Lanson, or even your

lecturer ? Most certainly, if you can show your reasons : independent thought, far from giving offence (as students often fear), is so rare as to be at a premium. Never let yourself be told what to think : but—it takes a lot of knowledge to erect a theory for oneself; most of the time, with the limited data at your disposal, the best you can do is to choose between the conclusions of those who are fully informed. At the worst, you can explain why you cannot accept any of the opinions you know of.

In these survey courses there may arise a special situation, where ' history of literature ' actually takes the place of the study of literature; this is the last of the cases I want to deal with. Your lecturer—and your examination—may deal with some authors you can only be expected to glance at (because of time), or you cannot obtain, in the libraries at your disposal, at all. You see where the danger lies : this is hearsay about literature which you cannot turn into real knowledge. You must minimize the danger, by discovering early which among the books referred to in the course are considered important, and making sure of reading these (in an edition with sufficient explanatory notes, such as the *Classiques Larousse*, if possible).

But some of this hearsay matter is bound to creep into any course—when a source or influence has to be mentioned (perhaps not even a French one) because it has contributed to a set book; or where a whole phase of development of a genre is traced as a background to the study of one or two of its masterpieces; or (less legitimately) in trying to make a ' survey ' complete (which it never can be).

You must of course learn it, amplify it by any reading you are advised to do, and be ready to reproduce it on demand. But you should be able to recognize it for the substitute it is, and you should try to tie it up with some part of your first-hand knowledge, to which it will be useful, and put the emphasis on that.

To take an example : you may be given the history of French drama before the *Cid* (as you can find it, more or less accurately told, in many English editions of 17th-century plays). If, as well, you read a mystery play, or *Pathelin*, or *Les Juifves*, these at least will be oases of knowledge in the desert of hearsay; otherwise, do not consider you *know* anything about all that stretch of drama except titles and dates—labels with nothing in the bottle. But your impressions, to call them that, may give you some better idea of where the *Cid* was original and where it was not, and build on to your knowledge of Corneille.

To sum up : respect only fact; and respect fact utterly, or all your work will be false. Pay attention to the judgements of all the established critics you come across, but trust no judgement except your own (if you think it deserves it). At least never work without it, and never be bullied into going against it.

Old French Literature

On your programme there will almost certainly be two or more Old French literary texts to be studied. These you should approach in the same sense of criticism as the modern texts you are called on to read. Your reaction to that remark will, I hope, be ' Obviously ' : it is not so obvious, however, to many students, and it is this fact that justifies devoting a separate section to medieval French literature.

Students often find that the lecturer who deals with, say, the *Chanson de Roland* spends almost all—perhaps even absolutely all—the class time considering the linguistic side of the work, and they content themselves with copying his approach. Now the lecturer often cannot help himself, because he is faced with a class which cannot understand the text in the original Old French. Insisting rightly on a thorough understanding as a necessary prior condition of literary study, he will first explain all the linguistic difficulties—and often have no time to pass on to the next step, the study of the content of the poem and the way it is handled by the poet. If you find that this happens, then *you* must do all the literary analysis yourself. It has to be done by you anyway, if it is to be of any value, for second-hand appreciation is as objectionable here as in the study of modern literature. And the literary analysis you should perform in the same way as for modern texts (see above, pp. 51 ff.) : you will choose those passages you consider most important for various reasons (characterization, motivation of plot, etc.) and then *write* your own assessments of them; nor will you forget to do the same for the text as a whole. (It is important to set down your *explications* in *writing* : it is the only way to track down the half-formed thought and to detect the weaknesses of your reasoning) If you work in this way, you will not be in danger of having, as many students do, to consider your medieval texts from the literary point of view for the first time when the examination paper is set before you.

Do this and there is no reason why you should not ' pass in Old French literature '. But you, as a reader of this book, will want to do more than just pass. This is how to do it.[1]

First, you should consider the ' background ' of your text to see how far it will enable you to reach a better understanding of it or closer sympathy with your author. This can, of course, be especially important with medieval texts, which spring from a society so very different from our own. The very attitude to writers, to authorship, to literary invention and originality, the transmission and multiplication of literary works, the nature of the audience, etc., all these factors differed in the medieval world and influenced the clerks as they wrote. To know, for example, how the *chansons de geste* were declaimed or chanted by the jongleur to a simple musical accompaniment before the public will help you to respond more sensitively to the way the audience is directly addressed in these poems, lines are repeated at intervals, and the same incident narrated several times over in a series of *laisses similaires*. It may even partly explain the structure of a poem, in that oral recitation is somewhat slow and the jongleur could recite only so many lines at a session. Similarly you will hold in mind the fact that, although the romances were read in private in, perhaps, *la chambre as dames*, silent reading could not have been common and this too would have its effect on writer and reader.[2] Again, the average writer of the middle ages does not seem to have been so greatly concerned as the modern author tends to be with his own individuality in the invention of his subject matter or of his literary method (there

[1] All these remarks concern a point of method normal where modern literature is concerned; but students faced with the study of medieval texts often seem to proceed by quite other methods—or rather by none.

[2] See H. J. Chaytor, *From Script to Print*.

were exceptions, and anyway he could not fail to impress his own mark on his work, of course). Indeed he would construct his whole work and the individual parts according to the precepts of the teachers of rhetoric in the contemporary schools. The portraits which are so common a feature of the romances are built up according to certain patterns; the lyrical and emotional monologues in these same poems will reflect contemporary rhetorical techniques; and so on. If, therefore, you are to consider your text, not only as it affects you in the twentieth century, but also as it probably affected its author's contemporaries (and a complete appreciation must include both aspects), then you will have to be acquainted with the literary principles accepted by the writer.[1]

Apart from this literary background knowledge you will usually need to enquire into the nature of contemporary society, its intellectual, religious and moral aspirations, its educational and religious institutions—the importance of such enquiry differing of course, from text to text. Quite a brief study of the importance of the Church in medieval society, for example, and particularly the Church's role in education, would make much more comprehensible the medieval writer's concern with religious matters (even in the realms of romance, as in the case of the *Queste del Graal*) and the religious assumptions that underlie their consideration of what most people tend to-day to treat as non-religious, political matters. The greater importance attached then to morality is similarly to be explained; and it is important that you should be ready to respond to the idealism implied in so many works. The *Chanson de Roland* is far more than an account of bloody battle after bloody battle, which is all some students are capable of seeing in it.

After you have communed with your text and extracted from it all the nourishment you are capable of, you should therefore see if this sort of background study can help you to enrich your understanding and appreciation. It is, of course, important to keep this ' background ' in its place and not let it occupy the front of the stage.

To put you in the right frame of mind and give you a feel for

[1] See E. Faral, *Les Arts poétiques du XIIe et du XIIIe siècles*; and H. J. Chaytor, *op. cit.*

the period, you could start with a general account of medieval life such as you will find in Ed. Faral, *La vie quotidienne au temps de Saint Louis*, Joan Evans, *Life in Medieval France*, J. Castelnau, *La vie au moyen âge d'après les contemporains*. As a seriously minded student you will wish to go further and concern yourself with the mental and spiritual life of the period; for this read G. C. Coulton, *Studies in Mediaeval Thought* and, for the later middle ages, J. Huizinga, *The Waning of the Middle Ages*.[1]

But for many texts such general accounts are not enough, and you will need to read studies of certain specific problems raised by the particular book in question.[2] It should, for example, be unthinkable for a student faced with the *Chanson de Roland* or another *chanson de geste* to fail to read M. Bloch, *La Société féodale*. A work that takes for granted a certain state of society and the mutual obligations it places on its members must, at some point, be considered in the light of that society. Similarly a courtly romance such as the *Chastelaine de Vergi* may cease to strike even the most down-to-earth type of student as much ado about nothing, if he goes on to read something about the changing status of woman in aristocratic society during what Bloch calls the ' deuxième âge féodal', something about the troubadours of Provence and the trouvères of Northern France and some of the poems they—or at least the latter—wrote, and to study *The Art of Courtly Love*, a translation of Andreas Capellanus' *De Arte honeste amandi* made by J. J. Parry. As a last example, why should a man like Villon think he could interest his readers in the reflexions of a boisterous student on death and bodily putrefaction ? These are, to be sure, eternal themes, but you are more likely to enter into the spirit in which his audience read his poems if, from a book such as Huizinga's (already mentioned) or I. Siciliano, *Villon et les thèmes poétiques du moyen âge*, you know something of the misery they were acquainted with in war, pestilence and destruction. You will not have

[1] Later in your course you can go on to the lengthy but excellent work of H. O. Taylor, *The Mediaeval Mind*.

[2] Titles of such works can usually be found in *A Critical Bibliography of French Literature*, Vol. I, *The Mediaeval Period*, ed. U. T. Holmes *et al*; and R. Bossuat, *Manuel bibliographique de la littérature française du moyen âge* and *Premier Supplément*, 1951–1953.

72

explained Villon, let alone explained him away, if you do this; but at least you stand a chance of sympathizing with him the more, and it is to be hoped that, even if you do not study literature with the main, or even the subsidiary, purpose of enlarging the sphere of your sympathies, such will in fact be the result.

In medieval France literary works were not written solely, or even mainly, in the vernacular. There was a vast output of Latin works, and, since the writers we are concerned with would have been educated in Church schools—and therefore educated in Latin—the influence of medieval Latin literature on French cannot be ignored. Helen Waddell's *The Wandering Scholars* is good in this connexion, together with her *Medieval Latin Lyrics*. Both have been reprinted by Penguin Books.[1]

For many, especially those who are intuitive rather than intellectual in their approach to the arts, the graphic and plastic arts provide an entrée into the Middle Ages. Literature was not kept separate from the other arts : just as miniaturists illustrated manuscripts, so the strange creatures of the Bestiaries can be seen fashioned in stone at cathedral entrances, Arthurian heroes grace the northern doorway of Modena Cathedral, King Arthur himself figures in the cathedral of Otranto, and so on. This suggests a study of reproductions of medieval art as an approach to medieval literature : odd hours spent gazing at, say, the illustrations of the first part of Bédier et Hazard, Volume i, will never be wasted. The student who wishes to go beyond this has many volumes of reproductions at his disposal, not to speak of such works of criticism as Réau et Cohen, *L'art du moyen âge et la civilisation française* and those of Emile Mâle. To see, in line, the elegance of the pictured heroines of medieval romance is, for some, to appreciate for the first time the new, civilized attitude to women shown in so many romances; to see, in late medieval art, the Christ of Pity, the Pietà, the Madonna of the Cloak, God the Father weeping over His Son, is to appreciate a little more the religious mentality of Villon and his contemporaries, especially in their devotion to the Virgin Mary; to see the illustrations of the

[1] If you intend to specialize at all in medieval studies, you cannot afford to neglect E. R. Curtius' masterly work, *European Literature and the Latin Middle Ages*.

Danse Macabre and the statues of Death with a few rags of flesh hanging from the human skeleton is to experience in all its physical intensity the fascinated horror with which these same writers contemplated death and the putrefaction it brings . . .[1]

Your second line of approach should be the reading of further Old French works. You will delude yourself if you think you have exhausted the riches of medieval French literature when you have studied, say, the *Chanson de Roland* and Villon's *Grand Testament*. If you are given a course of lectures on the history of Old French literature, then of course, to be honest, you must read at least some of the works discussed. But even if you have to follow no such general course, you cannot afford to confine your attention to the two or three texts prescribed for the examination. To put the case no higher, you will not appreciate all the value of the *Chanson de Roland*, if you have not read some of the other epic poems of the period; nor will you form a true estimate of the taste of medieval audiences if you confine yourself to the *chansons de geste*. But, you may well say, reading Old French is a slow business and there is not time for further reading, except what I can cover in the anthology we use in class for language work. But there is a way. If you cannot go to the art galleries, you can derive much value from reproductions; and similarly, if you have not the time to read further works in the original Old French, you can at least read some of the many excellent modern translations or adaptations of medieval romances, plays, chronicles. There are volumes in the *Classiques Larousse* with extracts in the original and in translation from the *Chansons de geste*, the *Romans courtois*, the *Chroniques du moyen âge*, etc. There is, especially, the series of *Epopées et légendes*, published by Piazza, Paris. This contains translations into the beautiful modern French of Joseph Bédier : *Chanson de Roland*, *Roman de Tristan et Iseut*, *Châtelaine de Vergi*, as well as work from other hands. There are the little volumes of Jeanroy's series, *Poèmes et récits de la vieille France* (Paris, Boccard). There are the *Romans de la Table Ronde* as adapted by Jacques Boulanger; the *Roman de la Rose* in the modern version of André Mary, and many other works that have passed

[1] This kind of study has its dangers if pushed too far, but with caution you might read Helmut A. Hatzfeld, *Literature through Art*.

74

through his rejuvenating hands : *Erec et Enide*, the *Roman de l'Ecouffle*, etc. Here is ' further reading ' that is guaranteed to be a pleasure.

And, finally, knowing that there is no clear-cut break between the medieval and modern periods, you will always be on the alert to discover the connexions between Old and Modern French literature. I do not mean merely the ' survival of the medieval in Rabelais ', but rather the survival and revival of medievalism in modern literature and art. One of the clearest examples of the permanent importance of Old French literature lies in *amour courtois*. If for nothing else, medieval literature deserves our continual study because it introduced woman and man's love of woman as a serious literary theme : and that at least is a theme that seems still very much alive. When you study the Précieux and the salons of the seventeenth century and other writers of that period (e.g., Corneille in *Le Cid*), you should always have in mind the poets of courtly love and the *cours d'amour* of the middle ages with their special attitude to woman and man in his relations with her, their elaborate code of conduct and the subtlety with which they studied the dialectics of love. In the eighteenth century the romances and their doctrines were popularized in the prose versions of Tressan's *Bibliothèque universelle* and so made accessible to a wider public, while at the same time even novelists whose attitudes to women and love were the very reverse of courtly, Choderlos de Laclos, for example, continue to make the relation of the sexes the central theme of their fabulations. In this same century, again, Marivaux turned out play after play that concentrated on the delicate exploration of the subtleties of awakening love. And, of course, the story could be continued through the Romantics right up to this century.

You will be on the alert for the modern use of the medieval myth and ask yourself what is so vital in these myths that authors are so ready to use them to-day : not only in adaptations such as Henri Ghéon made of the *Vie de saint Alexis* in the *Pauvre sous l'escalier*, but also in more original works. Quite apart from the Gothic novel and the medievalism of the Romantics (read Hugo's *Mariage de Roland* when you read the *Chanson de Roland*)

75

and of an Heredia or Leconte de Lisle, you will see something of the vitality of the medieval when you consider Wagner's *Tristan und Isolde* or see Cocteau's film on the same theme, *L'éternel retour*; when you see his play, *Les chevaliers de la Table Ronde* : or, to keep in the Arthurian field, Julien Cracq's *Le roi pêcheur* which makes of the quest for the grail the symbol of the poetic mystery; or finally, to quote English examples, when you consider what the Arthurian romances have brought of richness to our own literature in Malory's *Morte Darthur*, in Tennyson, even in such a light-hearted book as T. H. White's *The Once and Future King*.[1] It is unnecessary to prolong such a list (and, anyway, the important thing is that *you* should be on the alert to discover such survivals and revivals); enough has already been said to prove the vitality of Old French Literature, its intrinsic value and its germinal influence to-day.

Reading and libraries

First, a few points in addition to what I have said about the reading of set books. In your own interest, buy the edition prescribed in the syllabus and do your main work on that—for it has been chosen as the most useful. In this matter of editions make full use of the facilities offered by the foreign book departments of the leading University booksellers. They are familiar with the prescribed syllabuses and accustomed to dealing with post orders. They frequently have second-hand copies available.

---

[1] In other fields the same filiation is to be seen. According to Sainte-Beuve ' La Fontaine est tout entier dans le *Roman de Renart* ' and Rostand's *Chantecler* is otherwise inexplicable; while in the same lineage there are Colette's *La paix chez les bêtes* and Kipling's *Jungle Book*. The allegory of the *Roman de la Rose* leads to Patrice de la Tour du Pin, and the *Vie de saint Thomas le martyr* to T. S. Eliot's *Murder in the Cathedral*. The Miracle and Mystery Play have been revived : Ghéon wrote the *Pauvre sous l'escalier* and the *Bergère au pays des loups*; Henri Brochet, the *Mystère de saint Edme l'exilé*; and, of course, modern miracles and mysteries have come from Péguy : *Jeanne d'Arc*, and Paul Claudel : *L'annonce faite à Marie* (a miracle) and *Le soulier de satin* (a mystery). Very many novels have been written with a medieval setting, of course, and these can be very useful in reconstructing the Middle Ages for you. Besides the 19th-century novels (e.g. Hugo's *Notre-Dame* and Scott's Waverley Novels), there are those of our contemporaries : Helen Waddell, *Peter Abelard*; Zoë Oldenbourg, *Argile* and *Pierre angulaire*, translated into English as, respectively, *The World is not Enough* and *The Cornerstone*.

Besides the edition you buy, there are others which, if you are wise, you will examine in the Library, and sometimes use. Learn to discriminate between them : some are less good than the one you possess, either because the commentaries are more elementary, or because they are out of date and have been superseded by later research. (Get the habit of looking for dates of publication). For many of the standard authors, there is the ' Edition des Grands Ecrivains de la France ' (Hachette) of the complete works—with correspondence, and also long biographical notices (now rather out of date, but serious and useful), the ' external ' history of each work (i.e., the circumstances of publication or performance), careful indications of sources (scholarly, but not necessarily complete now), and, in the last volume of each series, studies of the writer's style and language which can be of great help.

There are often recent ' critical editions ' of single works. A critical edition is one which aims at giving the most satisfactory text—usually the author's last revision, occasionally the earliest form printed—after considering all the known editions in which the book has appeared; indicates all the variants which the author has introduced, with their dates; summarizes and often reproduces the sources; and sketches the ' internal ' history—i.e. the development of the work, as far as we can trace it, from its first conception to its appearance in print, and its subsequent revisions—and the ' external ' history, with, often, the views of the earliest critics.

Some of this matter will not concern you as an undergraduate —details of the various editions and the reasons for the choice of text, for instance (unless there is something significant about the revisions, as there is in Ronsard and Montaigne)—; other parts, such as discussion of sources or of the author's meaning, may be more helpful than anything else on the subject.

The next stage to this is important to any self-respecting scholar, and often neglected; I would urge it even on Pass or Subsidiary students, for whom I personally would not make an obligation of reading much of the critical material I shall come to last of all (though not all teachers agree with me here). It is to read more of those authors who are represented in your syllabus

77

by one book or so each. The syllabus prescribes, say, a comedy by Molière, a tragedy by Corneille, or a few *contes* of Voltaire : but Corneille has left over thirty plays (19 tragedies, 7 comedies), Molière, nearly thirty comedies, and Voltaire, besides many *contes*, wrote an epic, several histories, treatises and pamphlets, and many plays (of unequal merit). Is it not an obvious precaution to sample at least a few of these, if only to see if your impressions derived from the set book still hold good ? Do not waste time on what you know are minor works, go lightly on editors' introductions and notes (though the commentaries of the *Classiques Larousse* type of edition may be helpful and sometimes indispensable). But try to acquire some knowledge of your own on which may be based, with prudence, some of those generalizations which are only to be condemned when they are baseless and second-hand.

If you are an Honours student there is more reading for you, particularly in the later years of the course. Whenever time allows, but at least for any book having an important place in the course, you should know the best of what has been written about it and its author—special studies (including the conjectural, the doubtful and the slightly cranky), general surveys of ' l'homme et l'œuvre ', ' background ' studies of artistic, social and political history, relevant parts of histories of the genre, the ' school ' or the period. The bibliographies provided by lecturers will make a beginning (sometimes much more, more than anyone ever gets through), but if you are interested and not merely dutiful you will want to search for yourself and see what else is available.

The first step is to scan the library shelves, not forgetting the ' latest acquisitions ' which are usually displayed in some special place; the second, to consult the library catalogue, which contains, under each author's name, cross-references to studies of his life and work. Another valuable resource, which most students neglect completely, lies in the rack of learned periodicals : the Honours student should make a point of running through at least the tables of contents of these—especially the *Revue d'histoire littéraire de la France*, *French Studies*, the *Modern Language Review*. Much of the matter is very specialized, naturally, but an occasional article, or book-review, will prove very much to the point (the important books often come out first as articles)—and one can acquire much merit by showing oneself up to date.

Beyond this point (and the obvious reference books,[1] dictionaries and encyclopedias; and the English literature and criticism to which, if books interest you, you cannot be indifferent) reading shades off into research, which belongs to the graduate stage. But a long essay, an undergraduate thesis or dissertation if you have to write one, brings you into this type of work; and here bibliography—the search for essential reading-matter you do not know of—must be taken seriously as the researcher's first, indispensable task. General manuals of bibliography exist[2]; you will find them in Bouvier et Jourda, *Guide de l'étudiant* or Rudler, *Les techniques de la critique*; and there are many special bibliographies in different fields. The librarians will be glad to help you in these problems.

In fact the serious student ought to be at home in his library and with the people behind the counter—or rather, his libraries; departmental, College perhaps, and University, and also the public libraries, the branch near his home, the central reference libraries of both his home- and his university town. Finally you should know that any book you cannot get at one of these can probably be borrowed for you, at little or no cost, by your University from another library.

You will always have to depend on libraries, but a scholar cannot be content with them alone. What we value we want to possess. Only your own library is available for ready reference, for the leisure hour, and for later years. Most students receive

[1] I have not mentioned ' manuals ' of literary history. They are hearsay knowledge and ready-made judgement in their most insidious form. As ' source-books ' for genuine *facts* (names, dates, quotations) they have their use; as critical interpretations, some of them (Lanson, P. de Julleville, Mornet) rank with the best. The plates of reproductions of Bédier et Hasard are invaluable for reconstructing the material background of literature.

[2] Lanson, continued by Giraud, *Manuel de bibliographie*; Thieme, continued by Dreher et Rolli, *Bibliographie de la littérature française de 1800 . . .*; Talvart et Place, *Bibliographie des auteurs modernes de langue française . . .*; Subject Index of Periodicals; *The Year's Work in Modern Language Studies* (Cambridge); the bibliographies in the *Revue d'histoire littéraire*.

grants, which are meant to cover all the necessities of their student life : books are far less luxuries than some of the things their money goes on.

I have mentioned the dictionaries you should possess, including the English one, and the grammar; buy copies of set books, of course. What else ? Complete and good editions, above all, of the authors who have really meant something to you, on or off the syllabus—the Pléiade editions are the handsomest and best edited at present, but unfortunately expensive, with flimsy paper and narrow margins (though this is perhaps not a disadvantage).

Reading on the scale I have indicated is an ideal, but an ideal to which you should try hard to approximate. You are studying a literary subject, and you are not fully literate if you are not constantly aware of the packed shelves of books crying out to be read.

By no means all this reading can be close reading, even of great authors. Some critical or historical studies repay close attention from cover to cover, but others prove fairly useless on investigation; many have parts deserving attention and others that can be skimmed or left. Complementary to the art of close reading is the art of skipping, and both must be learnt, for life is short. The first page to glance at in a strange work of scholarship is the table of contents—all the better if it contains chapter-summaries; the next is the introduction, the next, probably, the conclusion. Then, if you know what you want from it, you know if you will find it, and where.

What is worthy of close or fairly close reading is probably worth noting (not in the margin, if it is not your copy!). 'Reading without stilus or pen,' said St. Jerome, ' is dozing.' Notes preserve points for future reference, but they may even serve to fix them in the memory. They should have the same form as lecture-notes, except that they will probably include verbatim quotations, and should have full references (author, title, page) for future checking. Do not destroy reading-notes made in preparation for essays and exposés; make them legibly enough to be kept, and file them away in the appropriate folder. They may be more valuable than lecture-notes, if they come from a specialist;

and the written word can be summarized more easily and accurately than the spoken.

3. THE STUDY OF 'CIVILIZATION'

It is possible to derive profit from a book without thinking of the author's surroundings and way of life (as many centuries had to with such a work as the *Iliad*); but it was not produced in a vacuum, and to understand any work or period fully—or for that matter any language—would require a full knowledge of the history, thought and taste of the time and place to which it belongs.

Some educationists go much further, and argue that the study of these attendant circumstances is the real object of a course such as yours, and language and literature means to this end. They would give prominence to French history, geography, economics, law, administration, education, social structure and problems, political life; perhaps a history of the French colonial empire, certainly a short history of religion, philosophy, science and the fine arts in France.

How much of all this can or should go into your course is not left to you to decide. (You will probably have at least a course on political and social institutions.) It will appeal greatly to some, who are more interested in life than literature; and, when it is not done superficially or perfunctorily, it is worthy of a place—perhaps a very prominent place—in an Arts Faculty. Its techniques are rather those of History or Social Science—in fact the difficulty at present is that it is a ' bridge ' subject or series of subjects, not often expertly treated inside French departments, and not often treated within just the limits they would like, outside them. You, in any case, are not expected to learn the special techniques of History—you have enough to do to learn your own—and so you can but accept the results at second-hand.

But even if your interests lie elsewhere, you cannot do without this kind of (substitute) knowledge, if only as a background to your reading; for few of your authors were purely literary in outlook, and all showed some attitude (if only hostility) to some aspects of life around them. You need it also to fit you to converse with French people of your own intellectual standing, or before you can make much of a French newspaper.

F

The arts come in another category. At least some of them should make an immediate appeal to a lover of literature, and they are a part of civilized life. What you can learn of the arts in France, or as they influenced France, will throw light, too, on your reading (and conversely). Some of the spirit of Corneille and Racine comes out, far better than in the illustrations of their early editions, in the intellectually-composed paintings of Poussin or Georges de la Tour, or the rich but refined detail, geometrically ordered, in the gardens and Louis XIV rooms at Versailles. Marivaux' half-unreal world has affinities with the *fêtes galantes* of Watteau and the music of Couperin. The realist painter Courbet shows the same world as many nineteenth-century novelists, in the same spirit. Much ' symbolist ' poetry has the same aims as much ' impressionist ' painting, or the music of Debussy.

Be careful however; the most interesting relationships are rarely between exact contemporaries—Poussin is earlier than Racine, Corneille earlier than Versailles, Mallarmé than Manet or Debussy. Sometimes they are results not of a prevalent spirit but of a personal influence, where you would expect an older artist to influence a younger (as Delacroix and Wagner influenced Baudelaire).

This kind of comparison supplies very suggestive hints and illustrations; but it has its risks. It involves you in other people's generalizations, and in arts other than literature you may find them difficult to check by close study of the works.

Going Abroad

For understanding present-day France, this study of the world outside literature is easier—it is possible to find out by experiment what it means to live as the French live. Possible, and also indispensable, for printed attempts at explanation all become out of date rapidly.

Going to France is, then, an irreplaceable part of your study; you will have to go at least once during your course and you should go as often, and for as long, as you can. Live with a family if possible. There is not much value in holiday courses; they only bring you in contact with other foreigners. France is preferable to Belgium or Switzerland, for they have slightly different ' civilizations', and their French has its own peculiarities.

Obvious mistakes to avoid are moping in shy solitude, or spending your time with fellow-countrymen; or being swayed by a few unfavourable first impressions (often due to prejudice); or judging too confidently by your own scale of values (probably habitual rather than reasoned) without considering whether another scale is in force there, which may be as valid as yours (cuisine, for instance, ranks above plumbing). It is tactful to give France the benefit of the doubt while you are there—and respectful, in the presence of an older civilization than ours.

The study of life, including its most everyday forms, takes first priority while you are there. Conversation, from serious discussion to chat with the concierge, is more precious than reading or writing, which can be done elsewhere. If you are not lucky enough to live with a family, make the most of every contact.

You will find plenty of kindness if you deserve it, and if you fail it is likely to be through timidity in taking what is offered. Forget your halting French, forget self-consciousness, keep up your end of the conversation; try to make yourself interesting, and helpful if possible, in return for the interest and help you hope to find. Ask questions, for here is the prime source of the explanations for a hundred things you ought to realize you do not understand (though the answers will not necessarily be authoritative). Be a little wary of entering an argument, for you are at a great disadvantage. Probably you ought not to presume to argue on religion or French politics, though the opinions of French friends on these points ought to interest you profoundly.

Newspapers and public meetings will enlighten you on the questions of the day—and puzzle you; they need to be made the subject of your questions in conversation. Watch the Frenchman at home, in cafés, in crowds, on holiday. Go to Mass and to the Protestant *temple*.

Go, of course, to art galleries and museums, and places of architectural interest (and before you go, learn at least to distinguish romanesque, gothic and Renaissance styles : elementary illustrated manuals are easy to come by). Go to the theatre whenever you can find a good modern or a classical play; to French films, of all kinds; and, if music means anything to you, to such French music as you cannot hear at home. Money is the limiting factor here, and it will probably deprive you of acquaintance with the best of French cuisine and the great French wines.

It is not enough to come home with an improved accent and a wider range of expression. Not that you can hope to become French : with your tastes and outlook partly formed already, you would not be happy if you could. To know and judge justly is to be partly outside and partly in—to feel what it must be like to live and think as a Frenchman, to have enriched yourself by much that you have learnt from France, but to keep not necessarily the standards you started with, but standards of your own.

What I have been saying amounts to this : be alert to seize new facts, impressions and ideas, connect them with the knowledge and experience you have, and try to make a coherent pattern of the whole, always provisional and always expanding. And this, applied to all your work, is my last word in this section on the branches of French studies.

These studies are a unity, and that unity, in turn, must not remain a closed compartment. Have you compared the assumptions about the nature of tragedy or lyrical poetry, used in English or German criticism, with those used in French ? Have you met, in Philosophy, with discussions about meaning that have a bearing on linguistics or style ? Do your own preferences in plays, films, radio and novels agree with the standards you have come to accept in French literature ? Do you read news reports and leading articles with the same standards of evidence and logic you have learnt for history applied to literature ?

Discrepancies may call for adjustments inside the French field, not always outside it; but every discrepancy reveals compartments in your mind. A good mind is one that sees relationships—and all studies of the activities of men are related. You did not come ' in utter nakedness ' to French, or to any academic study; and you must be able to keep all your equipment handy, increase it all the time, and use it all.

84

EPILOGUE

1. *Revision*

Wise departments slack off teaching some time before an important examination. Whether or not such an allowance is made, you ought to spread your own preparations over a good deal of the last term.

Besides revision proper, there is the plugging of holes which for some reason remain unfilled. By all means look out for these, deal with them (as early as you can), leaving out, if anything, only parts of subjects you have tried and know you do not get on with, and then only when you may reasonably rely on an alternative question.

Revision is something different—committing to memory what earlier in the course has been committed to writing and put aside. I have tried to inspire you with disgust for pre-digested notes; but now, at the end of your course, you must digest for yourself what you have got together in notes and essays and try to put it into precisely the kind of form I have condemned. The difference is that this time it is material you have made your own, it contains your own considered choices between conflicting judgements, together with some interpretations you may believe original, some examples you have found for yourself. You half-know it already because you have worked on it : the additional effort of tabulating it will help. When you try to repeat it (verbally or in writing) do not worry about the words (never learn *words*, except in special cases) but about the facts, or ideas, and the thread that joins them—for if you hold the thread you can probably reconstruct a forgotten step.

For the essential bits of crude memory-work, draw up lists and charts and stick them up somewhere : author's careers, chronologies of genres, and so on. Say them over once a day. Collect and learn the quotations you hope to use for illustration. In examinations as elsewhere, unsupported statements carry little weight, and apt quotations make all the more impression because they are hard to produce. Only, while inexact quotations may be tolerated, bad French or bad prosody are worse than nothing. Metre and rhythm aid the memory with verse—if you can scan; with prose it may sometimes be wise to substitute a summary or a reference.

The last few days are for getting your body fit and your mind fresh, by exercise and sleep. At Oxford, undergraduates are advised to go home, or on walking-tours, for their ' schools weekend '. The best way to invite disaster is to burn midnight oil now. It simply is not true that anyone benefits from a last mad spurt. Better a little less knowledge and a cool head to make the most of it. Mental fatigue, and the worry and insomnia that go with it, are the likeliest causes of examination nerves and black-outs.

What you may do, when your body is exercised—and even an hour before the paper—is to take a last look at your notes, reading calmly and not trying, this time, to see if you know them. All tension is unprofitable now, until you see your paper; so have the strength of mind to cut it out.

2. *The ordeal*

If you avoid the malady called examination nerves—as you can, with a good conscience and self-discipline—you can feel confidence that a reasonable degree of ability and industry will bring a reasonably successful result; for the papers are set and marked with that intention. Should they contain an unexpected difficulty that upsets you, it will upset enough others to oblige the examiner to make proper allowances.

You should have made most of your mistakes, and acquired good habits and sound technique, in your class-work; for you will have little time for second thoughts. Correct, clear, economical English is of tremendous importance; so are the arts of understanding a question rightly and answering it completely, logically and methodically, without irrelevance and with good examples. These have been discussed under the *dissertation* ; the rules for that are the rules for the good examination essay.

Detailed points : You need not observe the order of questions; but observe, and indicate, any subdivisions of a question (the examiner's mark-scheme depends on them, and there is no point in annoying him). In translations and compositions, insert no explanations (they will be obvious), and leave no alternatives (the choice is up to you).

In the examination room the brain should be driven like a racing car—hard, but intelligently, sparing it when possible, to get the best out of it. When it has been all-out for an hour or so, give it a break by sitting back and thinking of nothing, or taking a stroll (for paper, ink or any other pretext). Never beat your head against a wall—move on to another question or another point, and let your unconscious get to work on the first.

The unconscious has an amazing memory, and will often solve problems left to it. As an examinee I always found it worth while to take each question of a paper in several stages— (1) jot down ideas, (2) rough out a plan, (3) revise it, (4) write it out, (5) revise—and pass on after *each* stage to a stage of *each* of the other questions in turn. I had to watch the clock most carefully : but a lot of loose ends had tied up by the time I came back to what I had left. At least make sure of having a last look at every answer after a spell of work on something else.

APPENDIX A

Dissertation

These plans do not compete with the model plans given in the works mentioned on page 33. There can never be one 'right' plan. Personality, experience, opinions, mentality, sense of style differ from person to person; and a student can rarely know all the facts or ideas which would be relevant to an exhaustive treatment of a topic. But there are right principles; and the attempt has been made here to show a variety of possible ways of applying them, and suggest how the coat might best be cut from the cloth available.

N.B. The questions in the Introductions are meant to be written up as questions (the answers to be found later in the *dissertation*). All other questions in these plans are to be dealt with and answered where they occur.

I

'Tout amusement inutile est un mal pour un être dont la vie est si courte et le temps si précieux' (J.-J. ROUSSEAU).

Introduction

[If the source is known (*Lettre à D'Alembert*) :]

    (*a*) Occasion of the letter.

    (*b*) Rousseau's thought, as made clear there :   [etc.),
good men honour their obligations (to society, family, which fills their time and brings pleasure;
only the idle need *amusement*;
he doubts therefore if any *amusement* is ' necessary ',
but asserts that any which is not ' est un mal '—
        e.g. the theatre.

[Otherwise, work out the thought by analysis :]

    (*a*) e.g. Does this seem characteristic of Rousseau ?

        (or : Life to-day seems even more rushed;

        or : Is this opposed to modern ideas about ' leisure ' ?)

(b) Why *courte, précieux* ?

Define *amusement* and *inutile* (both depend on his ideas about the purpose of life).

Stress *un mal*.

[Continue, in either case :]

(c) (i) What is *utile* in life ?

(ii) Is all else *un mal* ?

(d) Consult various philosophical views,

(i) present in Rousseau's mind,

(ii) which might modify his conclusion.

1. Fairly general agreement that

(a) the end of life is happiness (but of what kind ?);

(b) there are certain obligations (neglect of which brings unhappiness, in one way or another).

2. (=Intr. *d* i)

(a) Obligations : the claims of

(i) religion, which in its extreme forms preaches rejection of the world;

(ii) our fellow-men (or society)—18th-cent. *bienfaisance* ;

(b) Happiness : the claims of Self—

(i) wellbeing and security,

(ii) ambition,

(iii) ' gathering rosebuds '.

Rousseau probably accepted (a) ii and (b) i, and rejected the rest.

Your own conclusion on 2.

[We have found conflicting answers to our two questions (Intr. *c*). None of the views examined, nor any compromise between some of them, can be *proved* in the compass of a *dissertation*. You will have to advance your own, modestly, saying why it seems preferable, and avoiding if possible the 1st person singular—say e.g. ' Il paraît difficile de ne pas admettre . . .'

You should here have answered question (ii) and, partially, (i) : but on (i) there is more to say.]

3. (= Intr. *d* ii and *c* i)

The survey in (2) was incomplete.

(*a*) Following Rousseau, we have limited *l'utile* to moral good and material well-being. But what of :

the Beautiful (including disinterested creation or enjoyment of art) ?

the True (disinterested enquiry or study) ?

(*b*) Since Rousseau's time we have come to admit (apart from the above) :

the physical and psychological necessity of recreation; the moral and social usefulness of sport and group activities. [Omit the theatre, since Rousseau explicitly rejected it, and it would throw the *dissertation* out of balance to try to refute him.]

Conclusion

(*a*) Recapitulate ethical conclusion reached in (2) :

how strictly should we condemn pure self-indulgence ?

(*b*) But we have found several classes of *amusements* which are not *inutiles*.

(*c*) (To end off, e.g.) Rousseau was temperamentally a puritan. (or : However, the range of possible *amusements utiles* is very wide; it is a duty to limit the time and energy spent on them.)

II

' Corneille n'a pas le sens tragique.'

Introduction

(*a*) Dare we say this of the second greatest of French tragedians ?

(*b*) *Sens tragique* = feeling for *le tragique*, viz. an abstract quality, the essence of the genre called Tragedy.

(*c*) Is there such an essence ? Is it foreign to Corneille ? [All that follows depends on the range of knowledge at the writer's disposal. Let us suppose the minimum—one tragedy of Corneille and a little Shakespeare.]

(*d*) We shall seek enlightenment by comparing these.

1. Analyse the play(s) of Shakespeare.

What, in it (them), deserves to be called—or has been called

—tragic ? (Choose headings *ad lib.*, e.g. character(s), situation, dénouement, provided you consider only what is relevant.)

2. Analyse the play of Corneille under the same headings.

Conclusion
- (*a*) Put together the results of (1) and (2), trying now to attain abstract and general conceptions.
- (*b*) Corneille has all—or some, or none—of what makes Shakespeare tragic :
  he has other great qualities which do—or do not—deserve the same name.
- (*c*) Does he then deserve the implied censure of the title?

[Supposing now a fairly complete knowledge of aesthetic theory and literary history, it would take a book to include all that might be said. The wise writer will select a limited number of the points most useful to substantiate his own opinion.]

Introduction
- (*a—c*) as above.
- (*d*) What is Tragedy, in the concrete ? in the abstract ? What are Corneille's tragedies, in themselves ? in his intention ?

1 (*a*) Tragedy has appeared in Greece, Rome, Renaissance Italy, England, France, Germany. Very brief sketch of each type, stressing changes. A common essence is assumed (found also outside drama, e.g. novel). [All this could go under Introduction (*b*).]
- (*b*) Summarize attempts to define this essence—Aristotle, Renaissance theories, modern theories—under a few headings, e.g. function, emotions appealed to, situations, characters . . .
- (*c*) Attempt a conclusion for (1), stating what common ground has been discovered.

2. (*a*) Examine several plays, or aspects of plays, by Corneille ;
- (*b*) Quote what he has said about other theories, and his own —using, in both sections, the headings of 1 (*b*).
  Add perhaps (*c*) Limits of his knowledge and appreciation

of the tragic tradition; other influences helping to explain his work; and

    (*d*) Tragic effects observed in Corneille by modern critics, which he has not mentioned.

[Alternatively, 1 (*b*), 2 (*a*), (*b*), (*d*) could be rearranged under the subject-headings, taken in turn.]

Conclusion

    (*a*) How far is Corneille in conformity with the tradition ? (Possible answer: in presenting serious situations, involving elevated personages, and treated seriously.)

    (*b*) Is this enough to treat his Tragedy as a legitimate variant ?

    (*c*) The value of what he has given us.

APPENDIX B

Explication

These two *explications* are specimens, not models. Other teachers might find other things to say about the passages, and no student's exercise would be expected to include all that is here.

Passage I, in order to be complete, had to be rather long, and the *explication* is reduced to skeleton notes, sometimes in the form of questions (for you to answer). A good exercise might go lightly on some of the points in the last two sections, and concentrate on one, e.g. (*a*) Hermione's love and jealousy from the beginnings described here to the impending murder; or (*b*) the change of mood in the middle of the passage, and the subtlety of its treatment; or (*c*) the dramatic, emotional and poetic qualities of Racine's style and versification; provided that in all cases it starts from the text.

In II the treatment is fuller, because the matter may present more difficulty. Alternative lines of development are suggested, but something of each must be present.

Both specimens suppose that the context and author are known. It would be possible to take II ' unseen ', as a study of style : I would be less suitable, since important questions (e.g. of motive) could not be answered.

I

Je ne t'ai point aimé, cruel ? Qu'ai-je donc fait ?
J'ai dédaigné pour toi les vœux de tous nos princes;
Je t'ai cherché moi-même au fond de tes provinces;
J'y suis encor, malgré tes infidélités,
5 Et malgré tous mes Grecs honteux de mes bontés.
Je leur ai commandé de cacher mon injure;
J'attendais en secret le retour d'un parjure;
J'ai cru que tôt ou tard, à ton devoir rendu,
Tu me rapporterais un cœur qui m'était dû.
10 Je t'aimais inconstant, qu'aurais-je fait fidèle ?

Et même en ce moment où ta bouche cruelle
Vient si tranquillement m'annoncer le trépas,
Ingrat, je doute encor si je ne t'aime pas.
Mais, Seigneur, s'il le faut, si le ciel en colère
15   Réserve à d'autres yeux la gloire de vous plaire,
Achevez votre hymen, j'y consens. Mais du moins
Ne forcez pas mes yeux d'en être les témoins.
Pour la dernière fois je vous parle peut-être :
Différez-le d'un jour; demain vous serez maître.
20   Vous ne répondez point ? Perfide, je le voi,
Tu comptes les moments que tu perds avec moi !
Ton cœur, impatient de revoir ta Troyenne,
Ne souffre qu'à regret qu'un autre t'entretienne.
Tu lui parles du cœur, tu la cherches des yeux.
25   Je ne te retiens plus, sauve-toi de ces lieux :
Va lui jurer la foi que tu m'avais jurée,
Va profaner des Dieux la majesté sacrée.
Ces Dieux, ces justes Dieux n'auront pas oublié
Que les mêmes serments avec moi t'ont lié.
30   Porte aux pieds des autels ce cœur qui m'abandonne ;
Va, cours. Mais crains encor d'y trouver Hermione.

Context

Racine, *Andromaque* (1677). From the interview between
Pyrrhus, King of Epirus in Greece, and Hermione, who had been
betrothed to him, near end of Act IV.

Andromaque, the Trojan captive, has at last agreed to
marry Pyrrhus. Hermione still loves him; she has just ordered
Oreste to avenge her by killing him.

Pyrrhus has come to inform her of the marriage (his motives
do not concern us here). (Do not analyse the scene in detail.)
From her first reply he pretends to conclude that she never loved
him. This is her answer.

Allusions to be explained :

   tes provinces (3)
   d'autres yeux (15), *ta Troyenne* (22)
   foi . . . jurée (26), *serments* (29)

94

mes Grecs (5) her suite : the southern Greeks are often *les Grecs* in *Andromaque*, as if Epirus in the north was a foreign country; cf *nos princes* (2).

Sequel : what happens to H and P as a result (very brief).

Analysis

H refutes P's statement, makes a (surprising) request, and, when refused, dismisses him in anger.

A i Line 1   introduces refutation of his statement;
  ii Lines 2–10 prove her love by recapitulating all she has done;
  iii   11–30 perhaps she loves him still.

B i   14–16 Even though he marries A,
  ii   16–19 she asks for one day's delay (so that she may leave).
            (Transition : he remains silent.)

C i   20–24 She reproaches him with thinking only of A,
  ii   25–27 and dismisses him, reminding him that he is breaking his oath,
  iii   28–30 and threatening divine (and human) vengeance.
            (Nothing fuller is required in this section.)

Matter

Hermione, the phases of her emotions, their causes, her motives.

Her character : pride, therefore angry humiliation at her treatment (seen already II, i–ii, and here : *honteux, injure, m'était dû*).

But this pride is abandoned here : it was unseemly for a maiden to confess her love openly even when it was returned (find examples). Here H forgets reserve and even self-respect —something more than pride is hurt.

(A) She dwells on *herself* : what she has done for P, deserving gratitude and love in return; the tone is bitterly reproachful. The facts are selected to prove her point, and even forced—*dédaigné* (men she did not care for), *cherché . . . au fond de tes provinces* (she was sent—and Buthrotum is not ' au fond ' of Epirus), etc.

In (iii) she is carried away : the facts here do not serve her argument, but they are the climax of her suffering.

(B) With the abrupt change of subject goes (as will be shown later) a surprising change of tone.

Why the change ? to make a request. (Ostensibly : ' If the wedding is to-day, I shall not have time to leave. Do not ask me to endure this.') At face value, this hardly accords with H's mood.

Why does she make it ? 18 has a double sense. Delay is the only way to save P's life (without confessing her plot). The pretext is at the same time a last test of any better feelings P may have.

Why should she wish to save him ? Her own words (13), though spoken bitterly, revive her affection. (An important and fairly frequent source of pathos in Racine : cf. V, i, 1420–21; a famous example is *Bérénice* 1110–11.) (All this is made clearer by V, i. If Racine had found room immediately after IV, 5, for a scene between H and her *confidente*, it would be clearer still. Why has he not ?)

Transition : P fails the test. (There must be silences before and after ' Vous ne répondez point ? ')

(C) H gives up the attempt.

(i) She has watched him closely (common feature in Racine; examples?)—he has not even looked at her. Here for the first time she talks of *him*, not herself; but not quite objectively. She draws conclusions from his inattention, which revive her jealousy and anger.

(ii) The words of dismissal have a double sense : (*a*) Do what you intend; (*b*) do not forget it is a crime against me —and even the Gods.

(iii) The threat reverses the order : first the vengeance of the Gods, then hers. The threat is scarcely veiled (Phœnix at least understands ; see lines following this extract).

Source.—This situation occurs in no classical literature dealing with H. The final imprecation is the only part of the passage which has a literary source (Euripides, *Medea*, 623–26). How far is it a help to Racine ? What does it show of his mind and methods ? (*Medea* is not used elsewhere in *Andromaque*.)

Historical inaccuracies (may be noted if desired).—

2—3 No Greek girl could have spoken this. She would not have been allowed to choose her husband; she would only have been allowed to leave her parents' home for an immediate marriage. (Nor would the 17th century have allowed it : but it is not strictly true of H.)

30 Greek weddings were never solemnized in public at a temple altar (but all weddings in 17th-century tragedies are—why ?)

Manner

How these changes of tone are produced.

A (ii) is apparently a series of plain statements, simple sentences answering her own rhetorical question.

Rapid : each coincides with a line or couplet, with few internal pauses.

Forceful : parallelism of construction. The personal note : repetition of *j'ai*. Added force from *malgré* (placed before caesura, 4, and repeated, 5), and alliteration of *t*'s (hard sound, 8–10).

But 8–10 are a *rallentando* (parenthetical phrase, the only complex sentence, and the only figure of speech : *rapporterais un cœur*) leading to—

First climax, a passionate summary of section ii (10) : antithesis, bold telescoped grammar (as if careless speech). A question, unanswered, implying more than statements could.

(iii) Full flood of emotion, ending with second climax (13) : long sentence, with main clause reserved to end, and only one pause (*ingrat*) in three lines. Force of *cruelle*, *trépas*, at ends of lines; *tranquillement*, *encor*, at caesura.

In whole division : *tutoiement* (its implication; only here in this scene—where else in the play?); the vocatives, *cruel* (1), *ingrat* (13) (cf *perfide* below, 20, and *bouche cruelle*, 11) : what is their special (weakened) meaning in 17th-century lovers' language ? is it not transcended here ?

B is slower and calmer : more breaks, especially in first line (not agitated—simply to hold up the pace); the run-over in

14–15 is not complete *enjambement*. *Coupe* of 16 gives great stress to *j'y consens* and *du moins*.

Return to *vous* and the formal *Seigneur*.

A touch of irony ?—*la gloire de vous plaire*.

But 14 suggests that the fault is less in him than in her destiny.

Stress on *un jour* (19).

C is bitter and passionate again. *Tutoiement* returns : *perfide* (20).

  (i) Sentences begin with *Tu . . . Tu . . .* (commenting on *his* behaviour). Alliteration of *t* (as before).

  Refusal to name Andromaque (jealous hatred) : *ta Troyenne* —cf. *d'autres yeux* (15) and H's earlier speech in this scene. Rather bold hyperbole : *comptes les moments*.

  Very bold figurative use of verb (for the 17th century) : *parles du cœur*.

  (ii) Completely colloquial style of 25 (as often in Racine), except for *ces lieux* (conventional poetic plural).

  Very rapid first hemistich (4 ' mute ' *e*'s).

  Va repeated at beginning of lines and sentences (26–27),—so also *jurer . . . juré* (26), *Dieux* (27–28).

  (iii) 30–31 repeat the sense of 27–29, but replace *les Dieux* by *Hermione*.

  31, the final climax. Prosody : two stressed monosyllables; principal caesura displaced; then stress on *encor, Hermione*.

  (Why does she speak of herself, here only, in the third person ?)

The ' source ' in Euripides : has it suggested any words, any features of style ? Has anything that seems suitable been rejected?

Commentary on language

Explain *mon injure* (6) (suffered by me)

    un cœur (9) (why ' un '?)

    infidelités, bontés (4, 5) (sense of plural of abstract nouns)

    vous serez maître (19) (do as you will)

    je . . . voi (20)

    un autre (23) (not *une autre* : see annotated edns.)

The metonymies *ta bouche* (11), *mes yeux* (17), *ton cœur* (22) (is anything gained by not saying ' tu ' or ' je '?)

A rather excessive use of *yeux, cœur* (cf 9, 15, 24, 30), here as throughout *Andromaque* (cf. several variants replacing these words). Unpleasantly artificial ?—a common tendency of the time. But this passage is unusually direct (*je, tu* : few figures of speech).

Conclusion

Range and flexibility in a highly stylized medium (restricted rhythm and vocabulary), enabling it to rise to its greatest heights in moments of passion.

A vigorous, but economical and subtle rendering of strong emotion, both of its violence and of its capricious changes.

There is a complete *péripétie* here in embryo—H relents, is rebuffed, and hardens again.

(Lesson for the student : it is impossible to look too closely or too deep into the workings of the hearts of Racine's characters; his treatment is always more delicate, inventive and natural than it seems at first.)

II

Après le tremblement de terre qui avait détruit les trois quarts de Lisbonne, les sages du pays n'avaient pas trouvé un moyen plus efficace pour prévenir une ruine totale que de donner au peuple un bel autodafé; il était décidé par l'univer-
5 sité de Coïmbre que le spectacle de quelques personnes brûlées à petit feu, en grande cérémonie, est un secret infaillible pour empêcher la terre de trembler.

On avait en conséquence saisi un Biscayen convaincu d'avoir épousé sa commère, et deux Portugais qui en man-
10 geant un poulet en avaient arraché le lard; on vint lier après le dîner le docteur Pangloss et son disciple Candide, l'un pour avoir parlé, et l'autre pour l'avoir écouté d'un air d'appro-bation : tous deux furent menés séparément dans des appartements d'une extrême fraîcheur, dans lesquels on
15 n'était jamais incommodé du soleil; huit jours après ils furent tous deux revêtus d'un san-benito et on orna leurs têtes de mitres de papier : la mitre et le san-benito de Candide étaient peints de flammes renversées et de diables qui n'avaient ni queues ni griffes; mais les diables de Pangloss
20 portaient griffes et queues, et les flammes étaient droites.

Ils marchèrent en procession ainsi vêtus, et entendirent un
sermon très pathétique, suivi d'une belle musique en faux-
bourdon. Candide fut fessé en cadence, pendant qu'on
chantait; le Biscayen et les deux hommes qui n'avaient pas
25 voulu manger le lard furent brûlés, et Pangloss fut pendu,
quoique ce ne soit pas la coutume. Le meme jour la terre
trembla de nouveau avec un fracas épouvantable.

Context

Voltaire, *Candide* (1757). The hero and the Leibnitzian
philosopher Pangloss have arrived in Lisbon from Holland in
time to witness the earthquake.

This, like the *auto da fé* and the second tremor, are historic
(1755–6), though about six months intervened between each. The
san-benito (yellow robe) and *mitre* (pointed cap) are authentic;
that of C denotes recantation.

The other details are presumably fictitious—the crimes of
the victims, and the hanging (in order to preserve the life of P).

9 *Epousé sa commère* (the godmother of his godson): regarded
by the Roman church as within the prohibited degrees (but it
seems doubtful whether the Inquisition would have dealt with
this).

10 *Arraché le lard*: Portuguese Jews had been expelled or
converted in the 16th century; by refusing swine's flesh these two
showed they still observed the Mosaic law.

Short notes are required on *autodafé* (definition) and
université de Coïmbre.

Analysis

An account of the *auto da fé*.

A Introduction:

 i Lines 1—4 The ceremony and its purpose announced in
      general terms;

 ii   4—7 repetition driving home the points.

B Preliminaries:

 i   8—10 Arrest of three victims

 ii   10—13 and of C and P,

 iii 13—15 who are imprisoned.

C *The auto da fé* :
   i   15—20 C and P arrayed;
   ii   21—23 the religious ceremony;
   iii   23—26 the flogging and executions.

D   26—27 Another tremor.

[Matter and Manner.—What Voltaire thought about religious fanaticism in general and the Inquisition in particular we know from other sources; but discussion must start from this passage, where the remarkable thing is that there is not a word of overt judgement. The futility of the *auto da fé* is conveyed obliquely by the contrast of the first and last sentences (7, 26–7). There is no comment on its barbarity. Matter and Manner are, then, hard to separate—Voltaire's ideas are only present as our reactions to his apparently neutral presentation. I retain the division, which could however be neglected.]

Matter

The passage is pure narrative in appearance. The characters are no more than indicated. The art of Voltaire is to omit (*a*) all but a few bare statements and selected descriptive details, (*b*) all mention of facts or motives which might justify or excuse the ' wrong side ', and (*c*) all appearance of taking sides, of pity or of condemnation. (N.B. Two details of great ironical force appear only later, at the end of the chapter : '*prêché*, . . . *absous et béni.*')

Thus he misrepresents the purpose of an *auto da fé*, which was to defend the true faith, save the souls (though not the bodies) of heretics if they recanted, and, in this case, propitiate the divine wrath by an act of piety. He makes it absurd (5–7) not by false-hood but by omission.

He next renders ridiculous the crimes or heresies imputed to the victims (first referred to as *quelques personnes*, 5, as if their guilt were immaterial). To the philosopher of tolerance belief or unbelief are not crimes; at the same time he chooses the most trivial grounds he can find. He might have acquiesced in the punishment of incest (but by the State) : between godparents the relation is spiritual, and to him fictitious. He might have defended the relapsed Jews : but there is no need to defend men who merely choose not to eat a scrap of bacon. What P had said is omitted (though it has been related previously).

A whole step in the story has been suppressed by the significant words *huit jours après* (15). There was a trial, including (*a*) a serious effort to convince the prisoners of their error (cut out because too favourable to the Inquisition ?)—Candide apparently did recant—and (*b*) probably torture (cut out because it comes in the wrong place and spoils the climax ?)

Finally, the sufferings of the victims are not even described (23-6); there are two adverbial qualifications, but of a different nature. *A petit feu* in the introduction (6) is a neutral phrase (perhaps not accurate), though it does invite the reflexion that this is the cruellest way of burning. The arrests similarly are told without any detail (8s.).

Note also *le même jour* (26), which is false.

Thus, deft editing has produced a narrative which is objective and historical only in appearance. If we accept it, we have no option but to accept Voltaire's unstated judgement on it : incongruous solemnity, injustice, cruelty, futility.

[Here, develop further Voltaire's ideas.]

Manner

The sentences are fairly short, with no enumerations or accumulations of words; few subordinate constructions, never more than one to any main clause, except in the first sentence; no figurative language—apparently casual because so cold, but calculated, concise, with a few elegancies :

> variations between passive verbs and the active construction with *on* (4–5, 8, 10, 13, 15–16, 23–25);
> balance between the two parts of the first sentence—*les sages du pays* (periphrasis) = *l'université de C.* (direct), *n'avaient pas trouvé . . . ruine totale* = *est un secret . . . trembler, un bel autodafé* (direct)=*le spectacle . . . cérémonie* (periphrasis)—with variation of order and a kind of chiasmus of periphrases;
> variation and ellipse in the cumbrous details of the *san-benitos* —note *les diables de P* (19) = *du san-benito de P.*

None of the actors is described; the officials are not even named (whereas in the preceding chapter there was 'un petit homme noir, familier de l'Inquisition' and his *estafier*). Only one detail is concrete enough to make a picture—the victims' garb (too grotesque and picturesque to miss ?). But it is not mentioned that it was sulphur-yellow. There are no indications of colour.

Of the very few epithets used—all inexpressive with one exception (27)—one occurs twice (4, 22).

The other descriptive touches come under the heading of Irony, which is as prominent a feature as suppression of detail : it takes the form of apparent approval or admiration, leaving the contrast between subject and comment to enlighten the reader. It is rather laboured in the description of the dungeons (*extrême fraîcheur . . . soleil*, 14–5; which would seem agreeable in a warm climate). In the few other descriptive expressions it is revealed by juxtaposition :

un bel autodafé (4), and

en grande cérémonie (6, after *à petit feu*), announce the contrast between senseless cruelty and elaborate solemnity;

sermon très pathétique, belle musique en faux-bourdon (22–3) contrast similarly with the executions related in the next sentence. So again *fessé* (undignified word) *en cadence . . . chantait* (23–4).

In the last line, *fracas épouvantable* (emotive epithet) drops the neutral tone to point the contrast, at a distance, with line 7.

Conclusion

[The conclusion might well be devoted to Voltaire the reformer and philosopher; but as I included this passage principally as an example of the art of leaving things out, I suggest a summing-up on these lines.]

There are passages, even in *Candide*, where Voltaire speaks his mind openly, with tone suited to subject (see the sentences immediately following this passage). But eloquence is not his strong point. His great skill lies in the art of editing and twisting his case (sometimes dishonestly) so that, once presented, he need not argue it. This is greatly aided if there is an ironical discord between matter and treatment, which persuades us into the desired reaction—without *bel* (4), *autodafé* would not be half so grim. (Further examples of each device may be quoted.) Here both are combined, with devastating effect.

BIBLIOGRAPHY

These lists give full titles and other details of the books we have recommended. They do not claim, for obvious reasons, to include all the books you will need to use during your course.

1. BOOKS TO BUY

BAILLY, R., *Dictionnaire des synonymes*. Paris, Larousse, 1947. 15/3.

Concise Oxford Dictionary of Current English, adapted by H. W. Fowler and F. G. Fowler from the Oxford Dictionary; revised by H. G. Le Mesurier and E. McIntosh. Oxford, Clarendon Press, 4th ed. 1951. 15/-.

**Concise Oxford French Dictionary*, compiled by A. and M. Chevalley, Oxford, University Press, 1934. 15/-.

GRANDSAIGNES D'HAUTERIVE, R., *Dictionnaire d'ancien français*. Paris, Larousse, 1947. 16/6.

GREVISSE, M., *Le Bon Usage*. Paris, Geuthner, 6th ed., 1955. 45/-.

†MANSION, J. E., *A Grammar of Present-day French*. London, Harrap, 1919. 5/-, with exercises 6/6.

—— *Harrap's Standard French and English Dictionary*. Part I, French-English. London, Harrap, reprinted 1945. 55/-.

*—— *Harrap's Shorter French and English Dictionary*. London, Harrap, 2 vols., 1946. 35/-.

MAQUET, Ch., *Dictionnaire analogique*, répertoire moderne des mots par les idées, des idées par les mots . . . Paris, Larousse, 1950. 14/9.

Nouveau petit Larousse illustré, dictionnaire encyclopédique, ed. Claude Auge. Paris, Larousse, reprinted 1955. 34/3.

†RITCHIE, R. L. G., *Nelson's French Grammar*, London, Nelson, reprinted 1953. 8/6. (Out of print.)

†—— *Nelson's Third French Course*. London, Nelson, 1934. 8/6. (Out of print.)

* These are alternatives, if the complete Mansion is not bought.
† Alternatives.

II. BOOKS TO CONSULT

1. *The Study of Language*

BALLY, C., *Traité de stylistique française*, Geneva, 2 vols., 3rd ed., 1951.

BRUNOT, F., *La Pensée et la langue*. Paris, 3rd ed., 1936.

GODIN, H. J. G., *Les Ressources stylistiques du français contemporain*. Oxford, 1948.

HATZFELD, A., et DARMSTETER, A., *Dictionnaire général de la langue française du commencement du XIIe s. jusqu'à nos jours*. 2 vols. Paris, 5th ed., n.d.

LITTRÉ, E., *Dictionnaire de la langue française*. Paris, 4 vols. and supplement, 1881-3.

MANSION, J. E., *Harrap's Standard French and English Dictionary*. Part II, English-French. London, reprinted 1946. Supplement: English-French and French-English, by R. P. L. Ledésert, new ed., 1955.

New English Dictionary on Historical Principles, ed. Sir Jas. Murray.
10 vols. and Supplement in 13 parts. Oxford, 1888–1933.

ROBERT, P., *Dictionnaire alphabétique et analogique de la langue française.*
Paris, 1953 onwards (3 vols. issued).

WEIGHTMAN, J. G., *On Language and Writing.* London, Sylvan Press,
1947.

Prose Composition

BERTHON, H. E., and ONIONS, C. T., *Advanced French Composition.*
London, 1924.

RITCHIE, R. L. G., *A New Manual of French Composition.* Cambridge,
1941.

RITCHIE, R. L. G., and MOORE, J. M., *A Manual of French Composition.*
Cambridge, 1914.

Dissertation

BOUVIER, E., et JOURDA, P., *Guide de l'étudiant en littérature française.*
Paris, 3rd ed., 1950.

MORNET, D., *Comment il faut composer et rédiger une dissertation française.*
Paris, 1939.

—— *La Littérature française enseignée par la dissertation.* Paris, 1936.

RAYOT, E., et ROUSTAN, M., *La Composition littéraire, psychologique,
pédagogique et morale.* Paris, n.d.

Old French Language

GODEFROY, F., *Dictionnaire de l'ancienne langue française.* Paris, 10 vols.,
1880–1902.

TOBLER-LOMMATZSCH, *Altfranzösisches Wörterbuch.* Berlin, 1925 onwards.

FOULET, L., *Petite Syntaxe de l'ancien français.* Paris, 3rd ed., 1930.

PATON, D., *Manuel d'ancien français.* London, 1933.

VORETZSCH, K., *Einführung in das Studium der Altfranzösischen Sprache.*
Halle, 1932.

Historical Philology

BOURCIEZ, E., *Précis historique de phonétique française.* Paris, 8th ed., 1937.

BRUNOT, F., *Histoire de la langue française des origines à 1950.* Paris
1905 onwards (13 vols. published to date).

BRUNOT, F., et BRUNEAU, Ch., *Précis de grammaire historique*, Paris,
3rd ed., 1949.

NYROP, Kr., *Grammaire historique de la langue française.* Copenhagen,
6 vols., 1904–30.

POPE, M. K., *From Latin to Modern French.* Manchester, 2nd ed., 1952.

SNEYDERS DE VOGEL, K., *Syntaxe historique du français.* Groningen, 2nd
ed., 1937.

VOSSLER, K., *Langue et culture de la France*, trans. A. Juilland. Paris,
1953.

WARTBURG, W. VON, *Évolution et structure de la langue française.* Berne,
4th ed., 1946.

Linguistics

BALLY, C., *Linguistique générale et linguistique française.* Berne, 3rd ed., 1950.
—— *Traité de stylistique française.* Geneva, 2 vols., 3rd ed., 1951.
BLOOMFIELD, L., *Language.* London, 1935.
BRUNOT, F., *La Pensée et la langue.* Paris, 3rd ed., 1936.
CRESSOT, M., *Le Style et ses techniques.* Paris, 1947.
DAMOURETTE, J., et PICHON, ED., *Des Mots à la pensée, essai de grammaire de la langue française.* Paris, 9 vols., 1911–50.
DAUZAT, A., *La Philosophie du langage.* Paris, 1948.
GILLIÉRON, J., *Généalogie des mots qui désignent l'abeille.* Paris, 1918.
GILLIÉRON, J., et ROQUES, M., *Etudes de géographie linguistique d'après l'Atlas linguistique de la France.* Paris, 1912.
GOUGENHEIM, G., *Eléments de phonologie française.* Strasburg, 1935.
—— *Système grammatical de la langue française.* Paris, 1939.
GRAMMONT, M., *Traité de phonétique.* Paris, 1933.
GUIRAUD, P., *La Stylistique.* Paris, 1954.
IORDAN, I., *An Introduction to Romance Linguistics, its Schools and Scholars,* trans. J. Orr. London, 1937.
JESPERSEN, O., *Language.* London, 1922.
MAROUZEAU, J., *La Linguistique.* Paris, 1950.
—— *Précis de stylistique française.* Paris, 2nd ed., 1946.
MEILLET, A., *Linguistique générale et linguistique historique.* Paris, 2 vols., 1921–36.
ORR, John, *Words and Sounds in French and English.* Oxford, 1953.
PALMER, L. R., *Introduction to Modern Linguistics.* London, 1936.
SAUSSURE, F. de, *Cours de linguistique générale,* p.p. A. Séchehaye et Ch. Bally. Paris, 4th ed., 1949.
ULLMANN, S., *Précis de sémantique française.* Berne, 1952.
—— *The Principles of Semantics.* Glasgow, 1951.
VENDRYÈS, J., *Le Langage, introduction linguistique à l'histoire.* Paris, 2nd ed., 1939.
WAGNER, R. L., *Introduction à la linguistique française.* Lille and Geneva, 1947.
WARTBURG, W. VON, *Problèmes et méthodes de la linguistique.* Paris, 1946.

2 *The Study of Literature*

Versification
BERTHON, H. E., *Nine French Poets.* London, 1930.
GRAMMONT, M., *Petit Traité de versification française.* Paris, 1924.

Explication
PHILLIPS, P. E., and DAVIES, J. B., *French Appreciation for Sixth Forms,* London, 1952.
RUDLER, G., *L'Explication française.* Paris, 6th ed., 1930.
SAYCE, R. A., *Style in French Prose : a method of analysis.* Oxford, 1953.
SCHLUMBERGER, B., *L'Explication littéraire.* London, 1951.

History of Literature
WELLEK, R., and WARREN, A., *Theory of Literature.* London, 1953.

BLOCH, M., *La Société féodale*, Paris, 2 vols., 1939.

BOSSUAT, R., *Manuel bibliographique de la littérature française du moyen âge*. Melun, 1951.

—— et J. MONFRIN, *Premier Supplément* (1949–1953) *au Manuel bibliographique . . .*, Paris, 1955.

CASTELNAU, J., *La Vie au moyen âge d'après les contemporains*. Paris, 1949.

CHAYTOR, H. J., *From Script to Print*. Cambridge, 1945.

COULTON, G. C., *Studies in Mediaeval Thought*. London, 1940.

CURTIUS, E. R., *European Literature and the Latin Middle Ages*, London, 1953.

EVANS, Joan. *Life in Mediaeval France*. Oxford, 1925.

FARAL, E., *La Vie quotidienne au temps de saint Louis*. Paris, 1924.

—— *Les Arts poétiques du XIIe et du XIIIe siècle*. Paris, 1924.

HATZFIELD, H. A., *Literature through Art*. New York, 1952.

HOLMES, U. T., et al. *A Critical Bibliography of French Literature*, Vol. I. *The Mediaeval Period*. Syracuse, new ed., 1947.

HUIZINGA, J., *The Waning of the Middle Ages*. London, reprinted 1952.

MÂLE, *L'Art religieux du moyen âge en France*. Paris, 3 vols., 1941.

PARRY, J. J., *The Art of Courtly Love by Andreas Capellanus*. New York, 1941.

RÉAU, L. et COHEN, G. *L'Art du moyen âge et la civilisation française*. Paris, 1935.

SICILIANO, I., *Villon et les thèmes poétiques du moyen âge*. Paris, 1934.

TAYLOR, H. O., *The Mediaeval Mind*. 2 vols. New York, 3rd American ed., 1919.

WADDELL, H., *The Wandering Scholars*. London, 7th ed. reprinted 1938.

Bibliographies

DREHER, S., et ROLLI, M., *Bibliographie de la littérature française*, 1930–39. Geneva, 1948–9.

GIRAUD, Jeanne, *Manuel de bibliographie littéraire pour les XVIe, XVIIe et XVIIIe siècles français*, 1921–1935. Paris, 1939.

LANSON, G., *Manuel bibliographique de la littérature française moderne* (XVIe, XVIIe, XVIIIe et XIXe siècles). Paris, 1921.

Subject-Index to Periodicals (British). London, The Library Association.

TALVART, H., et PLACE, J., *Bibliographie des auteurs modernes de langue française* (1801–1927). Paris, 12 vols., 1922–1954.

THIÈME, H. P., *Bibliographie de la littérature française de 1800 à 1930*. Paris, 3 vols., 1933.

The Year's Work in Modern Language Studies, ed. for the Modern Humanities Research Association. Cambridge, annually from 1931.